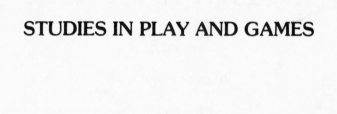

STUDIES IN PLAY AND GAMES

A COMPARATIVE STUDY OF THE PLAY ACTIVITIES OF ADULT ·SAVAGES AND CIVILIZED CHILDREN

LILLA ESTELLE APPLETON

ARNO PRESS

A New York Times Company

New York — 1976

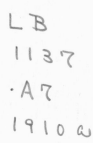
Editorial Supervision: SHEILA MEHLMAN

———◆———

Reprint Edition 1976 by Arno Press Inc.

Reprinted from a copy in the
  University of Illinois Library

STUDIES IN PLAY AND GAMES
ISBN for complete set: 0-405-07912-5
See last pages of this volume for titles.

Manufactured in the United States of America

———◆———

Library of Congress Cataloging in Publication Data

Appleton, Lilla Estelle, 1858-1937.
  A comparative study of the play activities of adult
savages and civilized children.

  (Studies in play and games)
  Reprint of the ed. published by the University of
Chicago Press, Chicago.
  Bibliography: p.
  1. Play. I. Title. II. Series.
LB1137.A7 1976   370.15'3   75-35062
ISBN 0-405-07913-3

The University of Chicago
FOUNDED BY JOHN D. ROCKEFELLER

A COMPARATIVE STUDY OF THE PLAY ACTIVITIES OF ADULT ·SAVAGES AND CIVILIZED CHILDREN

AN INVESTIGATION OF THE SCIENTIFIC BASIS OF EDUCATION

A DISSERTATION

SUBMITTED TO THE FACULTY OF THE GRADUATE SCHOOL OF ARTS
AND LITERATURE IN CANDIDACY FOR THE DEGREE
OF DOCTOR OF PHILOSOPHY

(DEPARTMENT OF EDUCATION)

BY

LILLA ESTELLE APPLETON

CHICAGO
THE UNIVERSITY OF CHICAGO PRESS
1910

Composed and Printed By
The University of Chicago Press
Chicago, Illinois, U.S.A.

PREFACE

Whoever has listened at educational gatherings to interminable discussions as to whether high-school courses should consist of four years' work or six; whether colleges should regulate the work of secondary schools, or secondary schools condition the work of colleges; whether promotions should be made once a year, or twice, or four times; where, in the curriculum, languages should be introduced; how much time should be given to purely "cultural studies," to manual training, and to arts; whether sciences should supersede the "disciplinary" studies, and so forth, and so forth, *ad infinitum*—whoever, we say, has listened to these endless disputations beginning nowhere and ending where they began, can hardly have failed to exclaim, "There must be some basis for the decision of all these points, which has never yet been reached, some ultimate controlling principle, to which all minor questions of form and content, of quantity and distribution, must be referred!" That such a principle is brought into clear and complete definition by the study here undertaken is not claimed by the author; but it is believed that it makes some real advance toward the discovery of such a principle.

If the comparison of phylogenetic and ontogenetic play activities has taught us anything, it is that physical and mental life are so closely correlated that the type of the one cannot be dissociated from the type of the other *in any individual*. Hence any art of instruction, to be adequate to the situation, must likewise change in type from individual to individual, as well as from age to age. This statement of the principle, as a mere statement, is, perhaps, not startlingly original; but it would be startling indeed to find a school curriculum conforming to it.

The difficulty in the way of such detailed adaptation is not so much in the failure of educators to comprehend the need, as in ignorance of how to meet the situation. Recognizing the inadequacy of past methods of instruction, they have added subject after subject to the school curriculum, in the vain hope that each new addition would overcome the deficiencies of the past. The analysis of play activities into their elements, however, and a determination of what elements predominate at different ages suggest the hypothesis that adaptation of the curriculum to actual growth conditions consists, not so much in introducing new subjects or eliminating old ones, as in analyzing each lesson, in whatever book or subject it may chance to be, into its psychological elements and in emphasizing just those particular elements which call forth from the particular individual the strongest response at his particular period of development.

We regret that the original charts in which the various plays and games are analyzed in order to find wherein the attraction lies are not published with the manuscript, but it is believed that to the ordinary reader conclusions only will be of interest rather than a multiplication of minute analytical details. The different rubrics have, therefore, been merely named, and typical illustrations are given together with deductions, the charts themselves being reserved for a more comprehensive work.

The author is greatly indebted to Dr. G. Stanley Hall, of Clark University, and to Professor L. T. Hobhouse and Dr. Alfred Haddon, of London University, for encouragement to go forward and complete a study undertaken and continued in the face of many discouragements. Except for the generous appreciation of the persons above named, and the much-prized opportunity for study, afforded, during the past year, by a Senior Fellowship in Clark University, the following study would probably not have been published.

Sincerest thanks are also hereby extended to Dr. G. A. Dorsey, curator of the Field Columbian Museum in Chicago, for assistance in anthropological research; also to Dr. C. H. Judd, of the University of Chicago, for reading the proof and otherwise greatly assisting

THE AUTHOR

MARSHALL COLLEGE
HUNTINGTON, W.VA.
January 1, 1910

CONTENTS

"*In view of the facts herein presented, we conclude, then, that although a similarity certainly exists between the play of the child race and the child individual, especially with respect to somatic characteristics, yet a process of differentiation has been going on throughout the cultural period which has profoundly modified, not only the final product, i.e., the product found in civilization, but also all the intervening stages. It is our belief that this differentiation is shown to a slight extent in the physical organism itself, so that the physical body of the highest type found in civilization is somewhat more sensitive to stimulation than is the body of the highest type of savage. This opinion is not based, however, entirely upon the study of play, but partly upon a supplementary study on "Somatic Characteristics." The chief difference appears, however, in the intellectual aspect of their amusements, and is a difference not of kind but of proportions, or, as we may say, of emphasis. . . . . But this difference of proportions is not acquired in any given individual by living the life of a savage until the limit of his development is reached, then adding to that product something more, which extends development in ontogenesis to the point reached in civilization. The differentiation in parallelism is much more fundamental, reaching back to the beginnings of psychical life, and probably far back into the physical organism itself.*"—P. 74.

I

INTRODUCTION

References (superior figures) throughout the text are to works in the Bibliography at the end, where cross-references are given.

The following paper is submitted as a contribuion to pedagogy and also to genetic psychology. Its bearing upon pedagogy will be immediately apparent from its relation to the "culture-epoch theory"—the theory that the child recapitulates the psychical as well as the physical evolution of his race, and hence that his mental growth is best promoted by assimilation of the cultural products belonging to that stage of *race* development, which corresponds to his own [See page 75.] Its bearing upon genetic psychology is twofold and may need, perhaps, to be more clearly defined at the outset.

Relation to Pedagogy and Genetic Psychology

Professor Baldwin has already pointed out[4] that, through the invasion into psychology of the theory of evolution, we are no longer satisfied with a mere description of forms of thought characteristic of adult minds only, but we now demand a *functional* psychology, a knowledge of the processes and evolutionary changes by which the dim consciousness of infancy transforms into the intellectual strength of maturity. In physiological science we include the whole series of changes in development, from birth to somatic death, under the term "life history." In psychological science we comprehend the whole series of transformations in mental development, from birth to somatic death, under the term genetic psychology.

At least, this is the usual meaning of the term, its ontogenetic meaning, but it might with equal aptness be applied in its phylogenetic sense, that is, to the development of mind *in toto*, including the whole series of evolutionary changes, if there be such changes, from the first premonitions of animal mind and the lowest of savage types, to the highest psychological products of the most civilized peoples. It is with this double meaning, including both the ontogenesis and phylogenesis of psychic manifestation, that the term genetic psychology is here used.

The paper here presented is an attempt to make a beginning of an unprejudiced study of the actual mental characteristics of some of the lowest of savage tribes with a view to finding whether their mental life does or does not reveal any definite types similar to those found in ontogenetic development. Is there, for example, a phase of phylogenesis which corresponds to that period of childhood when hunger for sensations seems to be the dominating impulse? Is there a period when the imaginative fancy controls the intellectual life? or when the critical judgment awakens to activity? or when philosophical speculation ripens? Is individualism a marked characteristic of any one level of phylogenetic development? or competition? or social feeling? or altruism? No doubt we shall find traces of all these characteristics at all points in the phylogenetic series, but in ontogenesis some of them certainly seem to become emphatic at pretty well-defined levels of development. Is this successive evolution of types discernible in phylogenesis, and if so, will they assist in any degree in constructing a psychological series which will fairly represent a continuous process of development from phylogenetic infancy to phylogenetic maturity?

The answers to these questions can be found in one way only—not by unwarrantable assumption that whatever is different from our own type or race is therefore lower; nor by speculative hypothesis, merely—but rather, and only, by direct investigation of the psychology of the savage and barbarous peoples themselves. Thus far, however, the light which such study would have thrown upon the whole subject of race psychology has been greatly obscured by the tendency, far too common, on the part of investigators, of lumping together all peoples of a comparatively low degree of civilization, especially the hunting peoples, under the one rubric "savages" and, too frequently, ascribing to *all* the characteristics of the lowest—a method quite as valuable, from the scientific standpoint, as it would be for Britons or Germans to lump together the peoples of the United States under the rubric "civilized," and to estimate the industries, ethics, religion, and general culture of the whole people by that of the civilized Negroes and Indians. In the following study on the play activities of savages the attempt is made to limit the investigation to a few of the simplest and least developed savage tribes known, in order to find the most elementary type of human adult mind now existing in its normal condition, to the end that it may be used as a basis of comparison, in the study of more advanced peoples.

The method of investigation is what has been called the "collective method," by which it is sought to find characteristics which really belong
Method of to the whole group, not merely those which are the result
Investigation of individual variation. The method has been adopted by
many investigators in child-study, and finds its largest illustration, perhaps, in the psychological studies directed by Dr. G. Stanley Hall, which have appeared from time to time in the *Pedagogical Seminary*,[25] and in *Studies in Education* edited by Professor Earl Barnes.[5]   In the two

volumes which the latter devotes to these studies, Professor Barnes attempts to ascertain (1) the varying types of mental life which characterize the individual in passing from infancy to early manhood and womanhood, and (2) the age at which these types become predominant. By a study of the child's attitude toward punishment he finds that the six-year-old child, if free to carry out his inclinations, would administer a wholly arbitrary and very severe punishment, entirely without relation to the motives of the offender, to the enormity of the offense, or even to laws existing for the express purpose of regulating such punishments. The same child at thirteen or fourteen years of age begins to take motives and mitigating circumstances into consideration and to temper severity with mercy in prescribing what the punishment shall be, while at sixteen years of age he will waive his personal inclinations and accept the punishment established by law. So, too, with regard to the critical judgment. In the little child it is almost lacking. He accepts blindly the fanciful story, the Santa Claus myth, or the fairy tale, without a question as to its truth, or the veracity of the narrator. A little later he asks for "true stories"; by the time he is twelve or fourteen years old the critical judgment has become active, and at sixteen he inclines to reject all evidence which does not stand the test of being "good authority."

To the writer it seemed possible, (1) that a phylogenetic as well as an ontogenetic series might present just such a continuous and perfectly normal series of changes from one mental attitude to another, at different levels of phylogenetic development; (2) that the viewpoint of the savages themselves might be determined, in many instances, by a method somewhat similar to that employed by the previously mentioned authors. In making this incursion into an unworked department of genetic psychology, the play activities of adult savages seemed to furnish a fruitful field of investigation as a starting-point, the conclusions in regard to which appear in the present paper.

It would have been extremely desirable to use exactly the same method of investigation, with respect to the psychology of savages, as has been employed in the study of child psychology, namely, the questionnaire method, by means of which the views of children are expressed in their own words. Unfortunately, this method is impossible of application with savages, who can neither read nor write. We are forced then to confine our investigations to such facts as are revealed in their institutions, customs, mythology, etc., and by studies of unprejudiced travelers and investigators and scientists. Our results will not, therefore, be quite so reliable as in case of the data obtained from children. Nor can we expect that the conclusions reached will be final—our knowledge of the primitive peoples is too incomplete for that—but even with such limitations, it is believed that we nevertheless have access to a rich field of investigation, hitherto neglected, and that even if the studies referred to fail utterly to establish the specific conclusions for which they were undertaken, they still have an ethnological value of their own, quite independent of the specific psychological questions involved. It must not be forgotten, however, that,

(a) Any psychological conclusions reached in the study of play must be verified and supplemented by studies of other mental phenomena of the same tribes, for example, the psychical characteristics of their art, language, mythology, science, music, ownership of property, and so forth.

(b) Intermediate and higher forms of civilization must be studied by the same method as the lower types here introduced, before any continuity of relationship can be affirmed between one group and another in the phylo-genetic series.

The study is inductive. We have steadfastly refused to be committed, mentally, to either side of the discussion, except as the evidence itself—in some cases leading to quite unexpected inferences—has compelled us. Hence, we have no thesis to defend. Nevertheless, for the sake of greater clearness of thought, the general conclusion of the study is given on p. vii. Minor conclusions will be found on pp. 74–83. It will be seen by a reference to those pages that our conclusions partly agree and partly disagree with the so-called recapitulation theory, if by that theory is meant entire agree-ment between racial and individual development. So far as somatic characteristics of play activities are concerned, very close though not perfect correspondence is found between the savage and the child. In the matter of organization of play activities, wide differences appear, while in the psychological characteristics of their play those qualities, such as, for example, rhythm, dramatization, and competition, which, with civilized children, are exceptionally strong in very early life, are also very strong with the savages—indeed, it would almost seem even more so with them than the children. On the other hand, the more purely abstract and intellectual phases of children's play are almost absolutely lacking.

It would thus seem that disparities in ontogenesis and phylogenesis appear in psychological development, in quite as marked a degree as Pro-fessor Lillie (see p. 75) affirms in biological development; and they tend to raise the question whether biological and psychological variations may not even stand to each other in the relation of cause and effect, or at least of correspondence. The possibility of such a relation has led to the formu-lation of what we have termed "the biological theory of play," for a wider application of which we must refer to a not yet completed study on somatic characteristics.

From what has just been said regarding lack of correspondence in recapitulation, it follows that we also fail to find complete confirmation of the culture-epoch theory, i.e., the theory that the subject-matter of instruction during any period of the child's development should consist of the cultural products of the race, which have developed during the period which is comparable to the child's stage of development. For while some phases of a particular stage of race development, as, for example, physical characteristics, might correspond quite closely to those of the child at some particular time, another phase of the same period, reasoning power, for example, might be far behind that of the child. Hence culture products, art, literature, etc., if used, should not be restricted to *any particular stage* of race development, as the hunting stage, or the agricultural, but should be gleaned from whatever source will awaken a keen response on the part of the child. His interest in the product will be the surest proof of its fitness for his use.

With this preliminary survey of the whole field of investigation we pass to a more definite consideration of our specific problem.

The first question which confronts us in the practical solution of our problem is the choice of specific savage tribes to be studied. In making this decision two conditions must be satisfied: (1) They must be low in savagery, even as compared with other savage peoples, in order that the simplest possible type may be obtained; (2) the groups to be studied must be chosen from such various locations, and conditions of environment, and must be so widely separated from one another, that if any common characteristics do appear, it will be because they are universal to all peoples of a similar degree of culture, not merely the result of circumstance and environment.

What Specific Tribes Shall Be Chosen?

In fulfilling the first of these conditions, the writer must be exonerated from all charges of prejudice in favor of such tribes as would exemplify or prove a pet theory, inasmuch as almost absolute ignorance of all of them, at the time when this study was begun, made a prejudicial choice impossible. Indeed, it is now believed that a somewhat different selection, for example, in the choice of the Eskimos, would have led to results much more striking than those here obtained. Some of the Indian tribes of California are possibly of a lower type than the Eskimos. Nevertheless as one Indian tribe was already selected from South America, it seemed better to retain the Eskimos in the phylogenetic group, for the sake of greater racial variety, and also because of the abundance and reliability of data which can be obtained concerning them.

Nor, under the circumstances, could we have any opinion as to whether the study here proposed would militate for or against the theory of onto-genetic and phylogenetic parallelism. It is the belief of the writer that the whole subject is, at least in its main contentions, somewhat in disfavor, at the present time, both with psychologists and anthropologists. To throw light upon the subject, *one way or the other*, has been the only controlling motive in the selection of data. Inadequacy of knowledge may make the conclusions incorrect, but inadequate knowledge is a difficulty inhering in every attempt at scientific investigation, and can only be met by further investigation, to stimulate which is one of the chief aims of this paper.

In estimating the culture of primitive races, we are learning more and more humility in the expression of opinion, as we are more and more led to realize how much ignorance and "the personal equation" have exerted an influence in the formation of those opinions. We will state, however, what have been the current estimates as to which tribes are considered lowest in civilization.

Karl Bucher names the following groups of savages, as being the lowest known tribes: the Forest Indians of Brazil; the Bushmen of South Africa; the Batuas in the Congo Basin; the Veddahs in Ceylon; the Mincopies of the Andaman Islands; the Australians; the Negritos of the Philippine Islands; the Tasmanians; the Kubus in Sumatra; the Fuegians of Terra del Fuego; the Botocudos of South America. Regarding them he says: "All the tribes involved in our survey belong to the smaller races of man-kind, and in bodily condition give the impression of backward, stunted growth." [7]

Morgan names the Australians and most of the Polynesians; [36] Tylor, the Australians and Forest Indians of Brazil. [61]

Spencer includes in his groups of lowest races the Fuegians, Andamans, Veddahs, Australians, Tasmanians (extinct), New Caledonians, New Guineans, and Fijiians. [58]

Grosse names the Australians, Veddahs, Bushmen, Yahgans, Eskimos, Andamanese, Botocudos, Tasmanians (extinct), Fijiians, the natives of Torres Straits, certain Brazilian tribes, the Bantus of South Africa, Pata-gonians, etc. [22]

Out of all these tribes, what specific groups shall we choose for our study?

In order to secure the greatest variety possible, both in race and in environment, suppose we choose a tribe from each of five continents—

from Asia, the Forest Veddahs of Ceylon; from Australia, the Central Tribes; from Africa, the Bushmen; from South America, the Canoe Indians of Terra del Fuego; from North America, the Eskimos.

Space does not permit to set forth here the details, most interesting though they are, of habitat, social environment, and personal characteristics of these peoples. Suffice it to say there is ample reason to believe that the tribes here named are not only extremely low in culture, but are also very ancient races.*

Having, then, thus briefly introduced our friends representing five different continents, one tribe from the Torrid zone, one from a tropical, one from a subtropical, one from a cold temperate, and one from a frigid zone—the first from the beautiful forests and parks of central Ceylon, the second from the semi-deserts of Central Australia, the third from the mountainous caves and uplands of central and southern Africa, the fourth from the bleak islands south of South America, and the fifth from the icy Land of the Midnight Sun—we are now prepared to analyze their characteristics, in order to discover whether there is, or is not, any prevailing type among these heterogeneous fragments of humanity. Among the most timid and unsocial of races, the most untutored, the bravest, the most treacherous and cruel, and the most hospitable of tribes, shall we find anything in common, beyond the two characteristics assumed in the beginning, namely, humanity and savagery?

In the search for psychological data, the play reactions have been selected for the initial study of characteristics, as being somewhat more tangible than purely mental phenomena, and also because much work has been done on the ontogenetic side. We shall not attempt to revise the results which have already been reached, regarding the laws revealed in children's play. We shall assume that these laws, so far as they have been formulated by Professors Hall, Barnes, Gulick, and others, are substantially correct. Our own effort will be limited to an attempt to extend the application of these laws to the race, as well as to the individual, and by so doing to determine whether any parallelism exists between the characteristics of the two. The savage tribes will be considered in the order in which they are named above.

* In an unpublished manuscript these points have been studied in detail.

II

ANALYSIS OF PLAYS OF SAVAGES

With the exception of a few simple games for children, which are excluded from this study, the Veddahs seem to have few amusements other than singing, and the dance accompanied by singing.
Forest Veddahs These latter are given only by men, and from the descriptions we gain the impression that even they are much more work than play. Hiller and Furness say of them: [26]

We saw no musical instrument at the village "where bugs are plenty," nor did we expect to find any musical tendencies in so silent a people; but when we asked the chief of the Rock Veddahs if they knew how to dance, he at once sat down on the steps of the rest house, and his four younger followers took their places in the roadway. Then the old chief sang in a dismal minor key, and the men, keeping step with the chanting, twisted and turned and stamped the earth alternately with the heel and the ball of the foot. Their arms hung loosely from their shoulders and swung with the motions of the body; their eyes were fixed on the ground at their feet, and their hair was shaken forward half obscuring their faces. The old chief nodded his head to the measured time of the dance, and clapped his hands, to which the dancers responded at times by voice or by clapping with their hands. There were various figures, and the change in the time, or a pause in the song, called for a new method of stamping or twisting. The four dancers seemed independent of each other, while following out similar figures, twisting in and out close together but never touching. At the conclusion the performers were perspiring profusely and seemed exhausted and quite dizzy, but at no time did they show any interest in the audience nor did they seem to realize that they were performing for the benefit of any one but themselves. The utmost solemnity was maintained throughout the dance; in fact we do not remember to have seen the slightest sign of mirth or laughter during our whole acquaintance with the Veddahs.

According to the Sarasins, the arrow dance of the Veddahs has a religious meaning. It takes place in a circle, about an arrow stuck in the earth. The performers move themselves continuously and slowly about the arrow, in a peculiar movement, without touching each other, each dancer making a half revolution, then another half, and so on. The feet move little, but the arms are actively swaying meanwhile, and the head swings with the arms. The hair is thrown about with the swinging head. They accompany their dance with informal singing, working themselves up into the highest nervous excitement, and becoming covered with perspiration as the dance proceeds.   At intervals they slap the body with their hands, the slap becoming harder as the performance continues, until it can plainly be heard some distance away.   One after another the performers fall exhausted to the ground, where they lie upon the back howling, perhaps, between gasps and trembling in every limb.[47]

These writers add furthermore that the dance is painful to look upon, that the onlooker becomes excited also in watching the game, and that to refrain from breaking in upon it constitutes a test of one's strength of mind. The participants are very earnest, and angry if anyone laughs.   Tennant "could never bring himself to permit the dance to come to its convulsive close."   The Sarasins believe, however, that while the dance has religious motives as its background, it is also employed as an expression of gratitude for any gift, inasmuch as, upon receiving the presents of the visitors, individual men began the dance again, and soon fell exhausted to the ground.   This method of returning thanks was especially noticeable in the case of one old man, who had received the much-coveted prize of an empty old bottle.   Hoffmaster also relates that a Veddah to whom a pocket handkerchief had been given tied it about his loins and danced in the manner described above.   In Nilgala a fire was sometimes built round the dance circle, when the hunt had been good, if the dance was to be held in the night.   Occasionally bows are placed around in a circle in place of fire.   Sometimes the dance is given in the hope of a better hunt, sometimes as a thankoffering for a good one.   Sometimes it is given in gratitude for the gift of a spectator.

Another author[47] describes a Wewatte dance of a similar nature but taking place in the night.   The moon had just risen; a brushwood fire threw its unsteady light upon the huts where the Veddahs lay, stretched out in disorder upon the ground.   All was still, when suddenly a Veddah began the first verse of a song.   It was a signal for all to follow, and together they rose up and began the weird, wild dance, accompanying it with hoarse deep tones resembling the death rattle, and striking their bodies with blows which answer the purpose of musical instruments, as an accompaniment to the dance.   Again they continued the violent exercise until exhaustion and dizziness overpowered them and they sank groaning and panting to the ground.

It is probable that such dances may also have the further significance of charms or exorcisms against wild beasts, as the Veddahs are known to have verbal charms of such a nature.[3]

Quite in keeping with this last idea is the *motif* of another dance of the Veddahs, but which the Sarasins think has been introduced from the Singhalese. In this the dancers hold branches of trees in their hands while they dance around the sick or dying friend who needs their friendly ministrations. The dance either summons the good spirits or drives away the bad one which is troubling the patient, and he is therefore able to recover.

But these serious-minded children of the forest have their pleasure dances also, as well as their hunting and exorcising and curative dances, and in these they appear in festive attire, that is, with leafy branches fastened about their waists. Unfortunately, we know little about them.

Closely allied to the dances are the improvised songs, such as that of the old woman to whom presents were given, in return for which she sang in a few tones constantly repeated, "The gentleman promised cloth, he has only given money," until he either gave more or dismissed his musician. The author adds that in this improvising of words and music, so similar to customs of civilized children, may, perhaps, be found the beginnings of poetry.[47]

Aside from the descriptions given above, the only other activity of which we have found any mention, which could by any means be regarded as a play activity, is the practice, not very common apparently, of discharging the arrows from the bow with the feet, instead of with the hands. It is difficult to see how this custom could have arisen, except in sport, unless it might, perhaps, be of some advantage in concealing a hunter from the pursued animal. One author, not a reliable one, however, mentions swinging from the branches of trees.

The play activities of *any* people probably do not represent the highest capacity which that people possesses. Some great emergency, or dire
Classification
of Play
Activities
necessity, or strenuous impulse is necessary to call forth the supreme effort which reveals the utmost of which human nature is capable. Plays do not, for the most part, furnish such incentives. They do, however, represent those powers of body and mind which have been habitually in use, and which are so well established that their exercise has become a pleasure and not a disagreeable task. It may be, therefore, that they represent the attainments of the people *as a whole*, even more truly than the sporadic cases of the few geniuses, who, intellectually, are much superior to their fellows. Is it possible, then, to classify play activities by any method which will make them a real criterion of race development, or a basis of comparison between different races?

They might, for example, be classified from the standpoint of *somatic characteristics*, noting, for instance, whether the physical activity of the play furnishes the chief source of enjoyment, or whether the intellectual elements of the play are the real attraction.

Somatic Type

Among the physical characteristics themselves, it may be noted, further, whether they are of the somatic type involving the use of the large muscles of the body as a whole, or whether they consist rather of the specialized order of activities dependent upon careful training and adjustment of the finer and more delicate muscles of the body, such as, for example, those of the fingers, or of the vocal cords.

It might be urged that any argument based upon such distinctions would fail, since, although such niceties of adjustment may not be found in the *play* of the Veddahs, they are found and habitually used in *hunting* activities, proving that the power of muscular control is really developed, even though it may not be used in play. It does not appear, however, even in the strenuous necessities of hunting, that the bow and arrow are used among the Veddahs with much exactness. Elephants are captured by shooting arrows into the feet of the animals until they are too lame to walk. But an elephant's foot is a tolerably extensive target. Bailey distinctly states that the Veddahs, though a hunting people, "are miserable marksmen," and although he repeatedly arranged shooting-matches in order to test their skill with bow and arrow, he never was able to find a person who showed much ability in this respect. We may probably safely conclude, then, that such skill is at least not sufficiently developed to make its exercise a recreation.

It must be distinctly understood, however, that the mere fact of indulgence in plays of the somatic type is of no significance whatever, if taken alone. The essential thing to note is that among the Veddahs *only* such plays are found. For example, there are no highly specialized finger plays at all comparable, in delicacy of movement, to piano playing, or even to the simple modern games of "crockonole" or "tiddledywinks," plays in which the result sought is dependent upon the perfect control of the small muscles of the fingers, the rest of the body being comparatively quiescent. Even those plays in which the arms and hands are chiefly employed, to the exclusion of the body as a whole—juggling, for example—seem to be also lacking. The question is raised at once as to whether this absence of high specialization has any biological significance. Does it mean that those muscles which come somewhat late under control in the development of the civilized child are not quite so fully developed, and not quite so finely organized in the lowest type of savages as with the civilized man? Or is

the absence of such plays a purely fortuitous circumstance, without significance of any kind? This question will be discussed farther on.

Secondly, plays might be classified from the standpoint of *organization*.
We judge of the young child, whose amusements are of the individualistic

**Objective
Type,
Organization**

type, consisting almost wholly of running, skipping, and
other purely physical exercises; who expresses his every
emotion, now in a spontaneous song, now in an impromptu
dance, now by hiding or jumping, but all without fore-
thought or plan—that is, without *organization*—and whose amusements
have little relation to his fellows, other than, perhaps, mere repetition of
their acts, that he is a less developed child, mentally, than another who is
full of initiative, who organizes his playmates into groups, for the purpose
of carrying out more complex designs, or of carrying them out more
effectively. We judge of a laborer, who goes at his task in a haphazard,
desultory, aimless manner, that he is a less intelligent man than another
whose work has been carefully planned and systematized. Shall we infer
that a people having only simple, unorganized, or little organized plays
of the physical-exercise type, is a less developed people intellectually than
another having well-organized and complex games, with rules to be strictly
followed, definite parts assigned to each player, definite ends to be gained,
and definite means for accomplishing those ends?

Thirdly, plays may be classified from the *subjective* standpoint, taking
into consideration the psychological elements which make them attractive,

**Subjective or
Psychological
Type**

apart from mere pleasure in physical activity. Such
elements are found in sensation, rhythm, mimicry, dramatization, competition or rivalry, and in intellectual skill or
alertness, etc. It is well known that in the individual child
the emphasis shifts from one phase to another of these various elements, in
his choices of games, during the process of his development, the imitative and
dramatic plays being chosen at one period, the competitive plays at another,
and so on. Which of these elements is most characteristic of the lower races?

Lastly, inasmuch as each of the three modes of classification named
above represents a genetic series, there may, possibly, be a gain in applying
all three tests to the play of the various tribes under consideration, with
a comparison of results. The latter method may be assumed to be the
safer one, since each series of results will be a check upon the other.

SUMMARY

1. *Somatic type.*—Summing up, then, the characteristics of the play of
Veddahs, and applying each of the three tests named above, the somatic
type is found to be *activity of the whole body.*

2. *Organization.*—The type of organization or the objective character-istics are:

(*a*) Individual play as in the case of the "thanks dance."

(*b*) The undefined group, as in the case of the arrow dance, which is sometimes performed by three persons, sometimes by many.

3. *Psychological type.*—The psychological characteristics are:

(*a*) Rhythm, as shown in the various dances, the movements of the body, swaying of arms and head, the nodding, clapping, and striking of the body, in the simultaneous movements of the dances, in the rudimentary poetry, in the repetition of phrases, and in singing.

(*b*) Spontaneity, as shown in the impromptu begging songs and "thanks dance."

(*c*) Mimicry should probably be named as the third characteristic, for, although not mentioned and apparently not noticed by the authors who describe the above-named dances, the arrow dance is undoubtedly a mimetic performance, in which the labored breathing, the "snorting like hippopotami," the "Leibeskräften Töne," the fall to the ground, the trembling, gasping, and occasional howls between the gasps, the death rattle, the convulsive spasms, and, finally, quiescence—all simulate the dying animal which the fatal arrow has brought down.

(*d*) The element of magic—the belief that in some mysterious way the performance in pantomime of the thing desired will bring about the actual event.

(*e*) Repetition.

SECOND GROUP

Concerning the amusements of the Central Australians we quote from Eyre: [17]

An amusement of the adults is a large bunch of emu feathers tied together, which is held out and shaken as if in defiance by some individual, whilst the others

Central Australians advance to try to take it out of his hands. This occasions an amusing struggle before the prize is gained, in which it is not uncommon to see from ten to twenty strong and lusty men rolling in a heap together. This is a sort of athletic exercise amongst them for the purpose of testing each other's strength. On such an occasion they are all unarmed and naked. . . . . At night dances or plays are performed by the different tribes in turn, the figures and scenes of which are extensively varied, but all are accompanied by songs and a rude kind of music produced by beating two sticks together, or by the action of the hand upon a cloak of skins rolled tightly together, so as to imitate the sound of a drum.

With regard to the dances Eyre says:

In some of the dances only, are the women allowed to take part, but they have dances of their own in which the men do not join.   At all times they are the chief musicians, vocal and instrumental.   Sometimes, however, they have an old man to lead the band, and pitch the tunes, and at others they are assisted by the old and young men indiscriminately. . . . . Being excellent mimics, they imitate, in many of their dances, the habits and movements of animals.   They also represent the mode of hunting, fighting, lovemaking, etc.   New figures and new songs are constantly introduced and are as much applauded and encored, as more refined productions of a similar kind in civilized communities, being sometimes passed from tribe to tribe, for a considerable distance. . . . . Of these amusements the natives are passionately fond, and when once . . . . induced to engage in them, there is no knowing when they will give over.   Dances are sometimes held during the day, but these are of rare occurrence, and seem to be . . . . connected with their ceremonial observations or superstitions. . . . . The dances vary a great deal among the different tribes, both as to figures and music, the painting or decoration of their persons, their use of weapons, and the participation of the females in them. . . . . The most interesting dances are those which take place at the meeting of different tribes.   Each tribe performs in turn, and as there is much rivalry, there is a corresponding stimulus to exertion.   The dances usually commence an hour or two after dark, and are frequently kept up the greater part of the night, the performers becoming so much excited, that notwithstanding the violent exercise . . . . they are unable to leave off. . . . . The natives of the Rufus and Lake Victoria (Tarru) have a great variety of dances and figures. One of these which I witnessed representing the character, habits, and chase of the kangaroo was admirably performed and would have drawn down thunders of applause at any theater in Europe.   One part of this figure, where the whole of the dancers successively drop down from a standing to a crouching posture, and then hop off in this position, with outstretched arms and legs, was excellently executed.   The contrast of their sable skins with the broad white stripes painted down their legs; their peculiar attitudes, and the order and regularity with which these were kept as they moved in a large semicircle, in the softening light of the fire, produced a striking effect, and in connection with the wild and inspiriting song . . . . led me to believe that the scene was unearthly. . . . .[17]

String puzzles are another species of amusement with them.   In these a European would be surprised to see the ingenuity they display and the varied and singular figures which they produce.   Our juvenile attempts in this way are very meager and uninteresting compared to theirs.[24]

We have also an account of an improvised dance observed in one of the coast tribes:

The Australians often invent new dances; for example, one who had been present at the capture of whales, by a party of whites, conceived the happy idea of imitating the proceedings in a dance, and to carry this notion into effect, a grand corrobory was resolved upon. An effigy of the whale was made, round which they danced, driving their spears into the figure.[17]

From the multitudinous dramatic and ceremonial dances of the Australians we select the following as typical:

About ten o'clock of the first day, it was decided to perform a ceremony. . . . . On occasions such as this, every man carries about with him a small wallet, which contains the few odds and ends that are needed for decoration in the performance of the various ceremonies. . . . . The men squat on the ground, and their wallets are leisurely opened out. There is no such thing as haste amongst the Australian natives. . . . . After some preliminary conversation, carried on in whispers, which had reference to the ceremony, the performers being instructed in their parts, and also in what the performance represented, a long spear was laid on the ground. One or two of the men went out and gathered a number of long grass stalks in which the spear was swathed, except about a foot at the lower end, which was left uncovered. Then each man present took off his hair waist girdle, and these were wound round and round until spear and grass stalks were completely enclosed, and a long pole about six inches in diameter and about eight feet in length was formed. Then, to the top of it, was fixed a bunch of eagle-hawk and emu feathers. When this had been done one of the men by means of a sharp flint—a splinter of glass if obtainable is preferred—cut open a vein in his arm which he had bound tightly round with hair string in the region of the biceps. The blood spurted out in a thin stream, and was caught in the hollow of a shield, until about half a pint had been drawn, when the string was unwound from the arm, and a finger held on the slight wound until the bleeding ceased. Then the down was opened out and some of it was mixed with red ochre, which had been ground to powder on a flat stone. Four of the Purula men then began to decorate the pole with alternate rings of red and white down. Each of them took a short twig, bound a little fur string round one end, dipped the brush thus made into the blood, and then smeared this on over the place where the down was to be fixed on. . . . . All the time that this was taking place, the men sang a monotonous chant, the words of which were a constant repetition of some such simple refrain as, "Paint it around with rings and rings" . . . . "paint the *Nurtunja* with rings." Every now and then they burst out into loud singing, starting on a high note and gradually descending, the singing dying away as the notes got lower and lower, producing the effect of music dying away in the distance. . . . . The decorated pole which is made in this way is called a Nurtunja, and in one form or another, it figures largely in the sacred ceremonies. . . . . As soon as the Nurtunja was ready, the bodies of the performers were decorated with designs drawn in ochre and birds' down, and then, when all was ready, the Nurtunja was carried by the Purula man to the ceremonial ground, and there . . . . the two men knelt down, the hinder one of the two holding the Nurtunja upright with both hands behind his back. It is curious to watch the way in which every man who is engaged in performing one of these ceremonies walks; the moment he is painted up, he adopts a kind of stage walk with a remarkable high knee action, the foot being always lifted at least twelve inches above the ground, and the knee bent so as to approach and, indeed, often to touch the stomach, as the body is bent forward at each step.

The Purula man who had been assisting in the decoration now called out to the other men, who had not been present, to come up. . . . . At this summons, all the men on the ground came up at a run, shouting as they approached, "whi'a, wha! wh'r-rr!" After dancing in front of the two performers for perhaps half a minute, the latter got up and moved with very high knee action, the Nurtunja being slowly bent down over the heads of the men who were in front. Then the dancers circled round the performers, shouting loudly, "wha! wha!" while the latter moved around with them. . . . . Then once more the performers resumed the position in front of the other men, over whose heads the Nurtunja was again bent down, and then two or three of the men laid their hands on the shoulders of the performers, and the ceremony came to an end. The Nurtunja was laid on one side, and the performers, taking each a little bit of down from it, pressed this in turn against the stomach of each of the older men who were present. The idea of placing hands upon the performers is that thereby their movements are stopped, whilst the meaning of the down being pressed against the stomachs of the older men is that they become so agitated with emotion, by witnessing the sacred ceremony, that their inward parts, that is, their bowels, which are regarded as the seat of the emotions, get tied up in knots, which are loosened by this application of a part of the sacred Nurtunja. In some ceremonies the Nurtunja itself is pressed against the stomachs of the older men. . . . . The whole performance only lasted about five minutes, while the preparation for it had occupied more than three hours. As soon as it was over the performers sat on the ground; the down was removed from their bodies and preserved for future use, and the Nurtunja was dismantled, the hair being carefully unwound and returned to its respective owners.[57]

The Australian is passionately fond of singing and indulges in it on all occasions, when happy, when sorrowful, when angry, when pacified, when full, when hungry, and when seated around his camp fire with his savage companions.

The songs are short, containing generally only one or two ideas, and are constantly repeated over and over again, in a manner doubtless grating to the untutored ears of a European, but to one skilled in Australian music, lulling and harmonious in the extreme, and producing much the same effect as the singing of a nurse does upon a child.[21]

Speaking of the songs of the coast tribes, Eyre says:

Europeans, their property, presence, and habits, are frequently the subject of these songs, and as the natives possess great powers of mimicry, and are acute in the observation of anything that appears to them absurd or ludicrous, the white man often becomes the object of their jests or quizzing. I have heard songs of this kind sung at the dances, in a kind of comic medley, where the different speakers take up parts during the breaks in the song, and where a sentence or two in English is aptly introduced, or a quotation made from some native dialect, other than that of the performers. It is usually conducted in the form of question and answer, and the respective speakers use the language of the persons they are supposed to represent. The chorus is, however, still the same repetition of one or two words.[17]

Of musical instruments the Australians are nearly as destitute as are the Veddahs. In some tribes sticks or boomerangs are struck together to mark the time, sometimes the ground is struck with a spear or piece of wood; "in one particular ceremony two short and bluntly rounded pieces of wood are used, which as they fall on one another, each being held in one hand, produce a 'clunk, clunk,' which closely imitates, as it is supposed to do, the sound of the croaking of a particular frog."[56] A rudimentary trumpet is also spoken of, which consists of a branch of gum tree hollowed out by insects, and which is used by placing it to the mouth and intensifying the sound by singing through the cavity.[56]

The play interest also finds expression in the ground-drawings and rock-paintings, many of which are connected with their sacred ceremonies, but not all. Spencer and Gillen say of them:[56]

Passing now to the geometrical designs, it may be noted that, so far as their form, and indeed, that of certain of the zo-omorfic and phytomorphic drawings is concerned, there is no distinction between them and certain of the drawings associated with ceremonial objects. They are dealt with separately because . . . . the latter have definite associations in regard to the totems, and have what the ordinary geometrical rock-drawings do not appear to have, a definite significance. By this we mean that the artist who drew them had no definite purpose in doing so. The natives, when asked the meaning of certain drawings such as these, will constantly answer that they are only play work and mean nothing.

Thus in the dance, in music, and in his paintings, the Australian spells out his mental type in letters which he who runs may read. If anyone doubt the truth of the inscription, let him compare it with the following character sketch, also from Spencer and Gillen,[56] our highest authorities on the Central Australian:

When times are favorable, the black fellow is as light hearted as possible. He has not the slightest thought of, or care for, what the morrow may bring forth, and lives entirely in the present. At night time, men, women and children gather round the common camp fires, talking and singing their monotonous chants, hour after hour, until one after the other, they drop out of the circle, going off to their different camps, and then at length all will be quiet, except for the occasional cry of a child, who, as not seldom happens, rolls over into the fire, and has to be comforted or scolded into silence. . . . . There is however . . . . an undercurrent of anxious feeling . . . . always lying dormant and ready to be called up by any strange or suspicious sound, if he be alone, especially at night time, in the bush, but on the other hand, just like a child he can, with ease, forget anything unpleasant, and enter perfectly into the enjoyment of the present moment.

SUMMARY

1. *Somatic type.*—The somatic type of the play characteristics of the Australian is activity of the whole body, as seen in the dance and in the trials of strength.

2. *Organization.*—The type of organization, or the objective characteristics are:

(a) Individual play; for example, in cat's-cradle or string games, and in certain of the dances.

(b) The undefined group, as shown in most of the dances and in the trials of strength.

3. *Psychological type.*—The psychological or subjective characteristics are:

(a) Rhythm, shown in the beating of sticks, slapping with the hand, striking together of boomerangs, beating the ground with spears or wood, in the "high-stepping" dance, in singing, in repetition of words.

(b) Spontaneity, as shown in the whale dance, and individual songs.

(c) Mimicry of animals and men, including almost every animal or stranger known to them.

(d) Dramatization of events relating both to their daily life and to their totemic ancestors.

(e) The element of magic—a belief that these dramatic representations will result in benefit to themselves or be pleasing to their totemic ancestors.

(f) Competition or rivalry, as appearing in their trials of strength, and in the dancing matches between tribes.

(g) Humor, burlesque, and a love for the grotesque.

(h) Repetition.

THIRD GROUP

With regard to the play activities of the Bushmen, we are even better informed than in the case of the two preceding tribes.   Stow writes:[59]

At one time . . . . the Bushmen had many games, in which they indulged in their leisure hours, to diversify the dance. . . . . There are still enough rescued from oblivion to show that they might be divided into three classes, of which the following may be given as illustrative specimens:

Bushmen

I. The "Nadro," or disguise. They appear to have had an almost passionate fondness for dressing themselves up in masquerading fashion, in the guise of some animal or other, so that it was not only in hunting and war that they simulated the wild animals, by which they were surrounded, but even in their amusements, their games, and dances.

One of . . . . the most popular [plays] was that in which the older women of the horde indulged, and which was specially called "*Nadro.*" They disguised themselves by fastening the head and horns of some wild animal upon their own, and so painting and enveloping the rest of their body in the hide of the beast, that they looked more like some wild or supernatural monster than a human being. . . . . This particular disguise was generally adopted in the evening, when one so dressed and carrying a small stick with which to make a rattling noise, would suddenly and unexpectedly come upon the assembled group of the horde, which always had the effect of startling the younger people, while even the old members would in the first impulse of the moment get out of the way of the rather unearthly looking apparition with no small degree of trepidation. As the alarm subsided, it was succeeded by bursts of merriment at the consternation and confusion which had been occasioned. They also disguised themselves in the same manner in some of their grand masquerade dances, when each impersonated some different animal and acted his or her part accordingly. The Australians and Eskimos also have plays similar to this.

II. Other games were such as required both skill and presence of mind, and were generally, if not exclusively, manly games. One of these might be termed the training game, although only experts would dare to join in it. . . . . Two Bushmen, each with a certain number of arrows, would take up a standing, sitting, or lying position opposite to one another, and then at a given signal let fly at one another, one after the other, with as great rapidity as possible, each with equal rapidity trying to avoid the shafts of his opponent. Sometimes the arrows were arranged in a row before them, or as worn in war or hunting, in a fillet bound round the head. The younger and more inexperienced were matched one against the other, whilst the oldest and most proficient members of the tribe would try their skill upon one another. When we consider that this game was played, not like some modern tournaments with half-severed and mock lances, but with genuine poisoned arrows, we may form some idea of the peril which accompanied it.

III. A third class of games also showed skill, but in these it was accompanied with a certain amount of legerdemain. . . . . One of these became so universally popular that it has been adopted and perpetuated among other tribes, by whom it is known as Bushman cards.

The following is a description of it as played by the Basutus:

Two or three people sit side by side or opposite each other, one of them picks up a stone or small piece of wood, all move their arms about in an excited manner, the one with the small piece of wood passing it with as much rapidity as possible from one hand to the other, so as to bewilder the other players, and then presents his clenched hands to his companions to guess where the wood is. If the guesser is mistaken the holder of the wood exclaims triumphantly, "Ua ya incha, kia ya khomo," in a kind of song or cadence, meaning, "You eat the dog, I eat the beef." In the opposite case, the player declares himself vanquished, when the guesser touches the hand containing the wood, saying "Kia ya incha, ua ya khomo," "I eat the dog, you eat the beef," and delivers the wood to his companion to do the same. The players will sometimes keep up the game for hours at their even-ing fires. The Bushmen also had a great number of imitative dances.

. . . . Miss Lucy C. Lloyd has given the following description of a game of skill played with a kind of shuttlecock, i.e., with a short stick with two or three feathers tied to its upper end and weighted at its lower extremity by a berry or a button attached to it. This is thrown into the air and beaten with another stick to keep it up. . . . . Miss Lloyd's Bushman authorities assured her that this is one of the old games played by members of their own tribe in their own land. This discovery is an interesting one as tending to prove that this popular game of English children is probably one (by being thus known to so primitive a race as the Bushmen) of high antiquity. . . . .

Some of their dances required considerable skill, such as that which may be called the ball-dance. In this a number of women, from five to ten, would form a line and face an equal number in another row, leaving a space of thirty or forty feet between them. A woman at the end of one of these lines would com-mence by throwing a round ball about the size of an orange, and made of a root, under her right leg and across to the woman opposite to her, who in turn would catch the ball and throw it back in a similar manner to the second woman in the first row; she would return it in a similar manner to the second in the second row, and thus it continued until all had taken their turn. Then the women would shift their positions crossing over to the other sides, and again continue in the same manner as before. . . . .

Another ball-dance was played merely by the men. The ball was made expressly for this game out of the thickest portion of a hippopotamus' hide, cut from the back of the neck; this was hammered when it was perfectly fresh until it was quite round; when finished it was elastic, and would quickly rebound when thrown upon a hard surface. In this performance, a flat stone was placed in the center upon the ground, the players or dancers standing around. One of them commenced by throwing the ball on the stone, when it rebounded; the next to him caught it, and immediately it was thrown again by him upon the stone in the same manner as by the leader, when it was caught by the next in succession and so on, one after the other, passing rapidly round the ring, until the leader or one of the others would throw it with such force as to send it flying high and straight up into the air, when during its ascent they commenced a series of antics, throwing themselves into all kinds of positions, imitating wild dogs, and like them making a noise "che! che! che!" but in the meantime watching the ball, which was caught by one of them when he took the place of the leader, and the game was again renewed. . . . .

The play was sometimes varied by two players being matched against each other, each throwing and catching the ball alternately, until one of them missed it, when it was immediately caught by one of those in the outer ring, who at once took the place of the one who had made the slip, and thus the play continued.

With respect to other amusements of the Bushmen, we find the following:

We have already seen the fondness of the Bushmen for disguising themselves in masquerading dresses, representing various animals, birds, and imaginary monsters. . . . . Beyond this, however, their powers of mimcry were wonderfully striking, and thus they were able not only to assume the appearance, but the action, manner, and cries of the animal they wished to personify, with extraordinary accuracy. It was this talent which enabled them to give such variety to their dances, an amusement of which they were passionately fond and in which they indulged on every fitting occasion. The universality of the custom was shown from the fact that, in the early days in the center of every village or kraal, or near every rock shelter, and in every great cave, there was a large circular ring where either the ground or grass was beaten flat and bare, from the frequent and oft repeated terpsichorean exercises.[59]

They had also a great variety of dances in which they indulged at new moon and full moon and at the approach of the first thunderstorm. There were dances for men alone, for women alone, for men and women together. There was the hunter's dance, the chain dance, the baboon dance, frog dance, bee dance, the dance of the chief, the dance of blood, and a grand national masquerade in which all the participants represented different birds and animals, and painted their bodies to help out the scenic effect. With these dances were musical accompaniments, music and words being fitted to the particular dance. The Bushmen also evolutionized their hunting bows into a musical instrument, the remote ancestor, possibly, of the modern harp, adding one string after another and then· a shell or gourd as a resonator, until it served as a fit accompaniment for their many songs and dances. Wallaschek quotes Burchell as saying that mere words are insufficient to describe the beauty of these songs and dances. They must be heard, they must be participated in. From these dances he derived as much pleasure as did the natives, "so quiet and orderly were they, no rude laughter, no noisy shouting, no coarse, ribald wit was there. Throughout it was a modest sociable amusement. . . . . Music softened all their passions, and thus they lulled themselves into that mild and tranquil state in which no evil thoughts approach the mind. The soft and delicate voices of the girls, instinctively accordant to those of the women and men, the gentle clapping of the hands, the rattles of the dancers, and the mellow sound of the water drum, all harmoniously attuned and keeping time together, the peaceful, happy countenances of the party, and the cheerful light of the fire, were circumstances so combined and fitted to produce the most soothing effects on the senses, that I acted as if the hut had been my home and felt as if I had been one of them." [63]

SUMMARY

1. *Somatic type.*—The somatic characteristics of the Bushman's play is activity of the whole body as shown in their gymnastic dances and nearly every one of the amusements of which we have any account.

2. *Organization.*—The type of organization or objective phase is:

(a) Individual play, for example, mimicry of animals.

(b) The undefined group, as in most of the dances and games.

(c) The pair, as in Bushman's cards.

(d) The double group as in the arrow contest.

3. *Psychological type.*—The psychological or subjective characteristics are:

(a) Rhythm.

(b) Mimicry of animals.

(c) Dramatization of events.

(d) Belief in magic.

(e) Humor, burlesque, and love of the grotesque.

(f) Real games as distinguished from mere play.

(g) Games of skill and competition.

(h) One guessing game.

(i) Since they have an extensive mythology, we may be sure that story-telling was one of their pastimes.

(j) Repetition.

FOURTH GROUP

The three tribes thus far studied are representatives of the Old World. We turn next to the New World to learn the characteristic

Yahgans   plays of the Yahgans and Eskimos. Of the former, Fitzroy says:[18]

Swimming is a favorite amusement of the Fuegians during summer. . . . . Men, women and children are excellent swimmers, but they all swim like dogs.

Swinging between branches of trees as our children do is also a favorite pastime, the ropes being made of strips of sealskin.

Grosse speaks of the dramatic efforts of the Fuegians,[22] some of which, he says, may be mimetic dances. Like the Veddahs, too, they also dance as an expression of good will and gratitude for a favor rendered them, as well as when asking for gifts.

Hyades and Deniker[27] state that sports are especially practiced during visits between different groups of Fuegians. After the visit is decided, at least six boatloads of Indians depart together, carrying about forty of the inhabitants who may volunteer for that purpose. Arrived at the end of their voyage, the men disembark, their faces painted, the forehead bound with a fillet of plumes. They advance toward the huts of their friends, holding their harpoons in their hands. The Fuegians visited hasten to meet the newcomers. One or two of the more elderly men advance to arrange with the newcomers for lodgment, etc. Greetings are exchanged and the edible berries are passed around.

They next propose to give themselves up to the wrestling plays which are always very much in favor. The play called "ka-la-ka" takes place between two natives placed in the center of spectators, who without mixing themselves in the action follow the game with the greatest interest. The players struggle, each seeking to raise his adversary and throw him to the ground. It is a spectacle which inflames the Fuegians who are always prepared thus to try the strength of their visitors. Sometimes the players become so excited and the maneuvers so brutal that fatal consequences result.

Another play is executed by two ranks of natives holding one another by the neck, and marching toward one another as they sing. At the moment when they come together the players lower the head, trying with all their might to break the line of their adversaries. When one of the lines is broken the gaiety is at its height by reason of the confusion produced among the players.

Ball is played with a ball made from the membrane of the foot of the gull. The players form a circle and throw the ball from one to the other.

They also take great pleasure in counterfeiting the cries of animals or in inventing burlesque scenes which occasion among the spectators explosions of laughter. "Quels que soient les jeux usités les Fuégiens y apportent un très vif intérêt; ils en parlent beaucoup le soir dans les huttes. . . . ."

It is extremely unfortunate that the songs of the Yahgans have not been preserved, but that they had many, there can be no doubt. There were songs of vengeance, and songs of mourning, medicine songs and songs for amusement. There were songs to the west wind, the north sky, the kelp goose, the loggerhead duck, and to many other of their familiar birds. They also enjoyed hearing European music, and sometimes joined in the songs of the sailors.[14]

Nearly every traveler who visited the home of the Yahgans, in the days which preceded civilization, speaks of their fondness for *mimicry*. The following from Darwin is typical:

They are excellent mimics. As often as we coughed or yawned, or made any odd motion, they immediately imitated us. Some of our party began to squint and look angry; but one of the young Fuegians (whose whole face was painted black, excepting a white band across his eyes) succeeded in making far more hideous grimaces. They could repeat, with perfect correctness, each word in any sentence we addressed them, and they remembered such words for some time. Yet we Europeans all know how difficult it is to distinguish apart the sounds in a foreign language. Which of us, for instance, could follow an American Indian through a sentence of more than three words? . . . . The Australians likewise . . . . imitate the gait of any man, so that he can be recognized.[14]

Of the more intellectual pleasures of the Yahgans, Spears, who, however, is a superficial observer, writes:

The missionaries say that within the limits of their knowledge, they were ready and logical thinkers. Sarcastic remarks and cynical observations abounded in their fireside conversations, as well as flashes of humor. . . . . He delighted in what civilized people call the higher pleasures, the joys of good stories, witty sayings, quick repartee, and he had almost unlimited opportunity for cultivating the faculties which gave him greatest pleasure.[55]

Evidently, however, they pursue these worthy pleasures in a manner characteristically their own, for Snow writes of them:

They are loud and furious talkers, and I soon found it was impossible to get myself listened to in any ordinary way. Accordingly, on one particular occasion when their noise was deafening, I took my speaking trumpet, and shouted louder than they. This answered. It made them delighted with my supposed skill, and it showed them that the white man could be equal to themselves. . . . . [54]

SUMMARY

1. *Somatic type.*—The somatic characteristic of the Yahgan play is activity of the whole body, for example, in swimming, swinging, and dancing, in the fighting plays, and in ball games.

2. *Organization.*—The types of organization or objective characteristics are:

(a) Individual play.

(b) Play in pairs.

(c) The double or matched group.

3. *Psychological type.*—The psychological or subjective characteristics are:

(*a*) Rhythm.

(*b*) Mimicry.

(*c*) Dramatization of events.

(*d*) Humor, burlesque, and sarcasm.

(*e*) Games as distinguished from mere play.

(*f*) Games of skill and competition, as shown in the ball games.

(*g*) Games of conquest, for example, the wrestling matches.

(*h*) Story-telling.

(*i*) Repetition.

FIFTH GROUP

We come last of all to the Eskimos. And here we discovered such a fund of information of undoubted authenticity that it seemed necessary
Eskimos to treat it by the somewhat more graphic method of the chart. We accordingly arranged a list of two hundred and fifty-five amusements of various kinds, practiced by adult Eskimos, excluding all those played by children only. Wherever the same play is mentioned more than once, it was entered on the chart more than once, pro-
Explanation of Chart vided it was mentioned by different authors, or by the same author as having been witnessed in different localities. The justification for this repetition is found in the belief of the writer that the mere fact of one game being observed more frequently than another implies that it is a favorite game, and therefore that it contains just those characteristics which indicate most clearly the mental type of the people who are attracted by them.

In the first column of the chart the reference to the book or article in which the play is mentioned or described was recorded. The second column gave the name of the author quoted, the third named the locality where the play was observed, and the fourth gave a list of the plays. Then followed an analysis of each of the plays, in which their most pronounced characteristics were indicated by crosses placed on the same horizontal line, under the rubric corresponding to that particular characteristic. These elements, which, combined, determine the peculiarities of the play impulse, were then grouped under three general headings: (1) Somatic Characteristics, (2) Type of Organization or Objective Characteristics, (3) Psychological Type, or Subjective Characteristics.

By Somatic Characteristics (columns v–ix) it was intended to indicate whether the play brings into activity the muscles of the whole body, or only parts of it, and whether the activity is of the more violent type, for example, the "tug of war," which indicates that the muscular activity itself is the chief source of enjoyment in the play; or whether the more quiet type of exercise predominates, which usually indicates one of two things, namely, either that the play is of the extremely childish type which goes with undeveloped muscles, not yet strong enough to bear violent exercise, or else that the muscular exercise is furnishing only a part of the pleasure, while perceptual or imaginative or constructive activity furnishes the other part. Making faces, and such games as tops and "buzz," would be examples of the first kind; the dramatic plays and the singing and dancing, performed for the entertainment of an audience, illustrate the second.

First General Rubric

In column vi, those plays involving parts of the body, rather than the whole, were grouped, as representing a somewhat more specialized type of play, but an analysis of the group shows that some of these really belong to the whole body group, inasmuch as the muscles of the entire body are tense and co-operative throughout the play, even though the chief activity may be located in the limbs. Take, for instance, the arm-pulling, pulling of arms and legs together, striking an opponent upon the back until he can endure the blows no longer, foot-pulling, stick-lifting (while another tries to hold it down), kyak racing, umiak racing—none of these have as an end the accomplishment of any delicate muscular work, or the securing of the fine adjustment of the arm or other muscles. A second division of the plays of column vi represents plays the specific purpose of which is the sensory effect. The "buzz," top, singing, etc., are representatives of this class. These and the dice games will be discussed elsewhere. But there is another subdivision of this group which does interest us just here. It includes the following games: juggling games, in which three or more pebbles are tossed one after the other, one being caught and tossed again, while the others are still in the air; another game in which the ball is thrown to the ground by the right hand, caught in the left, thrown with the left, and caught in the right, etc.; still another in which the ball is thrown with one foot to the other; shooting at a mark; throwing spears at a mark; a game similar to cup-and-ball, in which a piece of ivory, or more often the skull of some animal, is tossed and caught in some of its perforations upon a point of wood or ivory; drumming, which belongs to both the sensory and muscular group; a dart game in which the object is to pierce with a dart a perforation made in a piece of ivory, suspended from the top of the iglu;

violin (introduced by the whites and mentioned but once); a fish game, in which an ivory fish with a hole in one end is caught by a hook; a second dart game, in which the arrow-shaped dart is caught in the meshes of a net; carvings in bone, ivory, and wood; a throwing game in which the attempt is made to toss rings of grass so deftly that they will be made to fall upon and encircle a stake placed upright in the ground and at some distance from the thrower; tossing sticks so as to make them stand upright in the center of a spool-shaped block of wood; jackstraws and jackstones, both probably introduced. In all of these we have a type of muscular activity which does not properly belong to the soma as a whole, but to a specialized part of it. With these, success in the game depends upon delicate co-ordination of the muscles of the hand and arm—a careful measuring of the amount of force to be expended, so as to make it exactly correspond to the distance to be covered. Here then, we have an advance upon the Veddah and Australian type of play, which at least *suggests* the possibility that Eskimos possess a more finely organized nervous system, and muscular machinery under better control than is the case with Veddahs and Australians (see p. 11). The same conclusion with respect to superiority of development is again suggested in the fact that with the Eskimos, both in plays requiring violent exercise and in the "quiet plays" there is a far greater range of play activities, both in kind and number, than in the other groups studied. The following list, for example, of "parlor games" is no mean heritage for the social life of a savage, hunting people, living in a region so desolate and cold and unproductive that it is comparatively exempt from the incursions and outrages of so-called civilized peoples: "buzz," dice games, story-telling, cup-and-ball, dominoes (introduced by whites), singing, carving in bone, wood, and ivory, the roulette gambling games, mimicry, making faces, dancing, cat's-cradle, checkers (introduced by whites and mentioned but once or twice), ball-juggling, tops, dramatic recitations— these are some of the devices by which the savage host and his guests while away the long hours of the polar night.

By "Organization," (columns x–xviii), was meant the tendency to conventionalize a favorite amusement and to crystallize it into permanent form, which, in time, becomes "organized," i.e., has fixed

Second General Rubric rules to which the players conform. It has then become a "game" as distinguished from mere "play," and sometimes becomes a game of so great complexity that only an expert can get the greatest amount of pleasure from it. The most notable example of such a highly organized play of the somatic type is found, perhaps, in the American national game of baseball, the description of which in the *Young*

People's Cyclopedia of Games and Sports[7a] occupies twenty and one-half pages, including an enumeration of fifty-three rules governing the conduct of the game. Chess, with twenty-two rules and elaborate explanations, might represent the more psychological type of highly organized game.

We speak of civilized nations and societies as being "highly organized," and they undoubtedly are; but *if extreme organization in general is a characteristic of advanced civilization, little or simple organization might naturally be expected as a characteristic of slightly civilized societies,* and this is also apparently true.

But we are also told that play is a reflection of the instinctive, traditional, and conventional activities of a people, and we may assume, probably, without fear of the statement being challenged, that *the people living the more complex life will have a more highly developed repertoire of amusements.* It seems likewise probable that the unorganized form of play, without rules, is more primitive and elementary in type than the organized and conventionalized and regulated form of *games.* Now if the above statements be true, *we may find in a comparison of the simpler and more complex forms, and in the types of organization of play activities which represent the spontaneous and voluntary reactions of the participants, a basis of comparison with respect to the psychical development of our fivefold group; and likewise a similar basis with respect to phylogenetic and ontogenetic comparison.*

We must not assume, however, that because primitive forms of play are retained in use, the people who play them are therefore necessarily primitive. Among savage and civilized peoples alike it will always be desirable to have at command games simple enough for all to enjoy who may happen to be in the company, if the company be a heterogeneous one. Only the selected group will care for the highly specialized games. For this reason the primitive games will always be retained, even in the highly civilized countries. As a matter of fact, what we really find is that a highly civilized people has ten or perhaps a hundred simple games where a savage race has but one. What may be assumed, however, with certainty, as we believe, is, that if among any given people there are *only* extremely simple plays, of the cat's-cradle or roulette type, for example, it is because there are *only* simple-minded players, or at least but few of any other kind. On the other hand, if, in addition to these plays, there are others of a complex type, it is because some of the people have sufficient intellectual capacity to enjoy them. *The plays that are left* after the childish plays have been excluded—they are the ones which will have a story to tell us concerning the people whose tastes they represent. *Upon the evidence which they furnish and upon the relation which they bear to the former group*, we may, perhaps, base some ultimate conclusions regarding psychical development.

It is with this analyzing and sifting process in mind, then, that the term "Type of Organization" was made a second rubric on our chart of Eskimo play, while under it were included several subdivisions, whose function was to represent the various degrees of difference, or variation in form, which this process of organization or differentiation may take on. These subdivisions are:

1. "Individual Plays" (column xi), characterized by moderate motor activity, and little or perhaps no organization and no co-operation, cat's-cradle, for example, "buzz," and top, and the impromptu songs and dances. They are plays, rather than games. Some of them involve skill, as carving, drawing, and various feats with the kyak, and when highly developed *may* represent the highest art of any people; but with our primitive folk, these plays, whether they require skill or not, have either repetition and rhythm— a regulated form of repetition—or imitation, as predominant and very marked characteristics. All the dancing, singing, and drumming entertainments are very strongly characterized, both by repetition and rhythm. The "buzz," pebble-juggling, cup-and-ball, top, bull-roarer, hoop-rolling, tossing a ball into the air for the purpose of catching it, tossing a snowball from one foot to another, are almost purely repetitive. Carvings, drawings, mimicry, story-telling, pantomime, and cat's-cradle are imitative, and usually require more skill than the purely repetitive plays.

2. The "Undefined Group" (column xiii), characterized by a slight degree of both organization and co-operation. A small sub-group under this rubric, with the heading, "One and a Group," indicating that one person is the chief actor, while the others take a secondary position, differed from the preceding group of "Individual Plays" only in the fact that in the latter case the individual has an admiring audience, as, for example, in the drum songs and story-telling, the members of which sometimes join with him in responses of some sort. The elements of social feeling and co-operation make it a slightly more advanced type than the first group, though it is still play, not games. Imitation is a very marked feature. This group might, perhaps, be called *perceptual* play.

3. In the "Homogeneous" group, however, were placed such games as the following: tossing ball (from one to another), the dice games, shooting at a mark, foot-racing, spear-throwing, carrying weights, and other contests of strength, the roulette gambling games, the mock hunt, masquerades, cup-and-ball, leapfrog (introduced by whites), (toy) fishing, archery games, throwing contests, one or two ball games, blind-man's-buff, hide-

and-seek, toss on a walrus skin, tag, spinning (on a block of ice). The games under "Double Pair" (column xii) differed from these only in limitation of numbers. They were finger tracking (in pairs), one ball game (for women), one game of tag. Repetition appears about as frequently in this group as in the previous one, but it is not now the repetition of one's own act, as with tops or making faces, or of one's own words and tones, as in singing, or of motions, as in the dance; it is rather, speaking generally, a repetition of the act of some other person, who happened to start the game. Everyone playing does the same thing as the others, either simultaneously or successively. It is repetition a little more dissociated from self than is the case in the first group, while rhythm takes a very subordinate place. But the repetition here indicated is not mere repetition. Something else has come in to give to the play an additional zest. Each player not only tries to do, but to do as skilfully as possible, hence the term applied to such plays—"games of skill." The player consciously trains himself by repetition and effort to do better and better. In the first group the act itself was all-absorbing. Now *the manner of doing it* has become quite as much a matter of attention as the act itself.

Moreover, in many of the games still another element appears, namely, the desire not only to do skilfully, but to measure one's strength with that of others in the group, and to do better than anyone else can do. That is, rivalry, which scarcely appeared at all in the previous group, now begins to be an important element in the play. Motor activity is also a characteristic of nearly every one of the games, and most are *games*, not mere unorganized play. It will be seen, also, that most are more complex than the characteristic "Individual Plays."

4. Under the heading "Double Group" (column xiv), was placed a list of games—*all* games—in which organization is still more apparent. *Two undefined groups play against each other.* This means that the players must not only abide by the rules of the game, but they must act together. Social feeling has developed into conscious co-operation. Various kinds of ball games seem to be typical of the group, being mentioned ten times. Three games of tug-of-war appear, one of them a religious game, in which the two sides struggle to determine what kind of season shall prevail; umiak racing; one ring game, in which two groups of players form rings by taking hold of hands, each group vying with the other in racing for a distant goal, meanwhile revolving about the center of its own circle; chorus singing in two parts (belonging more properly to the homogeneous group); singing combats, in which two individuals are the chief actors but are supported by their friends. These complete the list. In most of

these the dominant characteristics are simultaneous repetition, rivalry or competition, and co-operation.

In column xii, a new element of organization appeared, namely, limitation of numbers. Under "Pair," and "Double Pair," are found the following games: wrestling, finger tracking, arm tracking, tracking of both arms and legs, foot pushing, the greeting ordeals of striking, wrestling, and knife-testing, boxing, rope-jumping (in pairs), checkers (introduced), head-pushing, hurdle-racing, foot-pulling, neck-pulling, stick-lifting (while another tries to hold it down), tug-of-war (by two), cards (introduced by whites, and mentioned but once), battering-ram, two ball games, twin tag (two persons tied together race with two others). It will be noticed that in these games *the element of imitation falls far into the background as a motive.* Repetition of acts remains, but added to it is "accommodation," i.e., to a changing situation. Moreover, the games have an intensity which did not appear before. It is not enough now to *surpass* in skill; the opponent must be crushed, conquered.

5. Next was listed what we have called the "Organized Game," because it approached so closely in its characteristics to what is termed organization in human societies, that is, games in which there is not only co-operation but differentiation of parts. Two are found which in a simple way suggest this class—battering-ram, in which two men take upon their shoulders two other men, their muscles stiffened, so as to remain in a horizontal position, when the opposing pairs make repeated rushes at each other, until one pair succeeds in knocking the other down. The second game is thus described:

This game is played at any season by men and women divided into equal parties, which are subdivided into pairs. Then a designated player starts off, pursued by the others, the players on the opposite side trying to overtake and touch him before he can touch the mate he was given from his own party. This mate strives to get within reach of his companion, the opposite side, meanwhile, using every effort to interfere between the two by running after the first and hindering the latter. If the player succeeds in touching his mate before he is touched, he wins, and another pair of runners come out from his side. If he is touched first by one of his opponents, he loses, and a pair of runners come out from among them and take his place.[41]

It would seem, perhaps, that the various football games and hockey ought to come under this heading, but so far as we have been able to find from any of the descriptions given, these games, *as played by the Eskimos,* are simply two unorganized groups of unlimited numbers playing against each other without captains, and without rules, except of the simplest sort. That this is the method pursued is suggested, at least, by occasional remarks of the writers describing them, that "football is played by young men and children," or "men, women, and children engage in the football games," which could not be the case if the game were played with regulations and with limited numbers, as in the American game of organized football.

A more condensed form of statement regarding the various characteristics of all the various groups described under "Type of Organization," might be expressed as follows:

SUGGESTIVE SUMMARY

1. CHARACTERISTICS OF INDIVIDUAL PLAY (COLUMN XI)

> Motor activity (moderate).
> *Successive* repetition of one's own act, i.e., imitation of self.
> Rhythm.
> *Sensory effects the chief aim.*
> No co-operation.
> Unorganized play, not games.

2. CHARACTERISTICS OF UNDEFINED GROUP (COLUMN XIII)

> Motor activity (marked).
> Successive repetition of *another's* act.
> Individual competition.
> Play subordinated to *games.*
> Imitation of self declining.
> Social feeling stronger, e.g., entertainment of groups in "play," as in singing.
> *Rivalry the aim in "games."*
> Self-training for skill.
> Slight organization and some co-operation.
> Effort.
> Greater complexity of type.
> Sensori-motor co-ordination for definite ends —a *fixed* problem in games, e.g., attainment of definite standard through definite means.

3. CHARACTERISTICS OF DOUBLE GROUP (COLUMN XIV)

> Motor activity(very marked).
> *Simultaneous* repetition.
> *Social feeling developed into marked co-operation.*
> Stronger organization.
> Games, not play.
> Effort strong.
> *Group, not individual competition the aim.*
> Greater complexity of problem.
> Sensori-motor adjustment to a *changing* problem, i.e., "accommodation" for the sake of co-operation.

4. CHARACTERISTICS OF
PAIR AND DOUBLE PAIR
(COLUMN XII)

> Motor activity (intense).
> Simultaneous repetition.
> Play rather than games.
> *Not co-operation, but conquest the aim.*
> Effort strenuous.
> *Limitation of numbers.*
> Strength and endurance tested.
> Adjustment to a changing situation.

5. CHARACTERISTICS OF
ORGANIZED GROUP
(COLUMN XV)

> Great motor activity.
> Repetition less marked.
> Co-operation *necessary.*
> Games—no play.
> *Group competition the aim.*
> Increased complexity in problem.
> Adjustment to constantly changing situation.
> *Slight differentiation of parts.*

We might now expect to see the process of organization carried one step farther and to find games in which organized rather than homogeneous groups play against each other, in which the parts are so much differentiated as to require limitation of numbers for each group, and in which the problem has become so complex so to necessitate a leader or captain or chief to direct the movements of the game. We should then have the typical "Team Game" (column xvi). But here we look in vain to find a single entry upon our chart. *Does it mean that such power of organization is lacking on the part of the savage tribes?* (See p. 12.)

In this study of the elements of organization, and in their relations to each other, we get glimpses of the genetic phases of play activities—various sequences in progression, which may be expressed, for example, as follows:

I. (1) An individual unit; (2) a homogeneous group; (3) an organized group; (4) a more highly organized group; (5) division of labor.

II. (1) Sensory plays; (2) perceptual plays, i.e., sensation in relation; (3) judgment of concrete relations; (4) judgment of abstract relations.

III. (1) Motor activity controlled by stimulus; (2) motor activity under voluntary control; (3) motor activity regulated and made conformable to activities of other members of the social group, i.e., under *social* control.

IV. (1) Repetition of self-activity; (2) repetition regulated, i.e., rhythm; (3) repetition of another's activity, i.e., imitation; (4) repetition with adaptation, i.e., "accommodation"; (5) repetition *subordinated to "accommodation."*

V. (1) Action motivated by sensory pleasure; (2) action motivated by social appreciation; (3) action motivated by individual aggrandizement; (4) action motivated by aggrandizement of the group.

VI. (1) Action isolated with reference to others; (2) action brought into relation to volition of others; (3) action for the purpose of excelling others; (4) action for the purpose of co-operating with others.

With respect to somatic characteristics, we find *activity extremely characteristic of every stage of development.*

Columns xvii and xviii served in a measure as a counter-study for columns x and xi, making as they did a very similar comparison from a slightly different point of view. In these two columns, all the unorganized plays were grouped together, and all the games were grouped together into columns by themselves, thus showing the relation, in numbers, of plays to games. They confirmed the results of the previous study, in showing that while the number of games was great as compared with the other tribes studied, the number of plays was much greater. The columns, then, which under the first two rubrics are thickly studded with crosses are those which indicate activity of the whole body, "Quiet" play, characterized by repetition and rhythm, i.e., singing, dancing, poetry, and drumming, "Individual" play, and play of the "Unorganized" type.

It has become apparent, perhaps, from the discussion of the first and second rubrics, that the "Type of Organization" is only a mental type after all. Yet there are some characteristics in which the **Third General Rubric** psychological elements are more apparent to the casual observer. *Could we dissociate from each other the psychological elements in all the plays, and regroup them, putting each type in separate columns, we might get a graphic representation, perhaps, of the relative frequency with which each occurs, and, further, we should have added an important clue to the understanding of the psychology of these savage peoples.* Such was the problem attempted under the third general rubric, "Psychological Characteristics" (columns xix–xxxi).

Of repetition we have already spoken as entering in one form or another into almost every play. What other features appeal most strongly to these adult Eskimo minds? Mere stimulation of the senses, motor, auditory, visual, or tactual? rhythm, dramatic imitation, the acquirement of skill, the love of the ludicrous, competition and rivalry, the fascinations of games of chance and of gambling, the supposed test of character furnished in the ordeal, the victories of courtship, the exercise of purely intellectual powers, the expression of religious tendencies?

Each of these suggestions was made the heading of a column, and under each heading, in most cases, several subheads served further to analyze the characteristics of the various plays, as well as to show the preferences of the players. Where several important elements entered into a play, as, for example, somatic activity, rhythm, and competition, an equal number of entries was made. Indeed, the number and variety of elements involved in the play—that is, its complexity—proved to be a fairly good indication of the higher or lower character of the type.

The first thing which impressed one in looking at the chart was the tremendous emphasis which sensory effects, motor, visual, auditory, or tactual, have in the play of the people. We find a fairly constant succession of crosses in all four of the columns. These results are, perhaps, not surprising, in view of the fact that sensory elements enter so largely into *all* play. But what may, perhaps, furnish an element of real surprise to one who has given no thought to the matter is that the effort to excel, the attainment of "skill," either in strength, endurance, ability, accuracy, imitation, memory, perception, or good-natured deception, has an equally prominent place (column xxiv).

Attention has already been called to the fact that repetition, either of one's own act or of that of another, is an almost constant element in all amusements mentioned.

"Rhythm" (column xx) and "Dramatization" (column xxi), were also largely represented, but probably not so generously as they deserve, inasmuch as many authors say in a general way that the Eskimos are passionately fond of burlesque, humor, singing, drumming, mimicry, or mimetic dances, without making a statement sufficiently definite to warrant an entry on the chart.

The column headed "Ludicrous Effects" (column xxiii), indicates that the Eskimos are certainly not wanting in an appreciation of pure fun. The plays include "insult songs," which, though they certainly can hardly be called "good-natured" fun, yet permit no trace of ill-nature to appear on the surface; comic figures carved in ivory; trials of strength with the purpose of showing the other fellow his inferiority; "stunts" such as walking in peculiar ways which others try to imitate; daring and amusing feats with the kyak; burlesque gymnastic performances; mimicry; comic songs, of which the Eskimos are said to be very fond; making faces, also a favorite sport; musk-ox hunts, in which the players dress themselves up in skins and then turn their dogs loose; masquerades in which they either so represent different animals, or else try to get a costume as grotesque as possible; ice-spinning, in which the booby of the party is placed on a block of ice and revolved as rapidly as possible, until he is overcome by dizziness; string games, i.e., performances in making all sorts of animals and objects after the cat's-cradle method; good-natured "chaffing" in conversation; practical jokes.

As to "Gambling Games," except in Alaska and about Hudson Bay, where the Eskimos have come in contact with whites and Indians, neither the number nor variety is very great, but we are told that in some localities the Eskimos are passionately fond of them and will even gamble away the last article of clothing, in which case the winner usually gives back at least a part of the clothing with the advice to "play more and lose less next time." The introduced games, cards and dominoes, are mentioned two or three times, but the favorite gambling games are (1) of the roulette type, in which a cup of musk-ox horn, or some substitute for it, is revolved rapidly, the person to whom the handle points when it comes to rest winning the stake; or (2) of the dice type, in which bones of some animal are dropped, the position in which they lie when they come to rest determining who has the stake.

At Hudson Bay a game similar to cup-and-ball is played as a gambling game. The skull of an animal is tossed and caught in certain definite positions upon a sharp point of wood or ivory. This seems to be a favorite play among nearly all of the Eskimos, but in some localities it has been developed into a rather complicated game of skill.

The only other gambling game found, until we reach Alaska, is a thrusting game in which a piece of ivory with a hole in its center is suspended from the top of the iglu. The players vie with one another in trying to pierce the hole with a pointed piece of ivory or wood.

Of the games described at Point Barrow, Alaska, Mr. Murdoch distinctly states that the Eskimos have but one gambling game—a throwing contest. We have not found it mentioned by any other writer. At Bering Strait and vicinity, however, the following are named: throwing at a mark; a net and dart game—the one who succeeds in sending his dart so as to have it caught in the meshes of the net wins the stake; throwing darts at a spool-shaped body with a hole in the center; throwing grass rings over a stake; another dart game; two games similar to jackstraws and jackstones. The following will serve as a type of the dart games:

This is played in the kashim by two or more persons, usually for a stake. The darts are small, short, and made of wood, largest at the point, and tapering backward toward the butt, in which is fastened a bird quill for guiding the dart in its flight. In the large end of the dart is fastened a sharp spike of bone, horn, or sometimes of ivory. The target is a small upright stick of some soft wood planted in the floor. This may be placed in the middle of the room and the players divided into two parties, seated on opposite sides of the target, or it may be placed on one side of the room and the players seated together on the other. In the former case a man is appointed to return the darts to the throwers and to give each player a counter when a point is made. Each player has two darts which he throws one after the other, and a score is made when a dart remains sticking in the target. Ten small wooden counting sticks are placed on the floor by the target, and one of these is given for each score; the side gaining the most of these counters takes the prize, and the game begins again.[41]

We have found no evidence that any of the gambling games have religious associations, as is the case with those of the Indians, unless the "chance" element itself may be considered a religious idea of an elementary sort like that associated with the "ordeal." Some of them may have been borrowed from the Indians, however.

A very interesting group of games is found under the heading "Ordeal" (column xxviii)—not large, but extremely significant. They are all games of contest, and the idea underlying all of them is, that whichever one wins in the struggle is not only the stronger but the better man.

First on the list are the "singing combats" or "nith songs," and here we shall give the description as related by Rasmussen, describing the customs of the East Greenlanders, who are probably the most primitive in type of the Eskimo groups;

Insult songs were the means the east coast Eskimos used to settle up all their differences. When two men had cause of enmity against each other, it was their mode of duel. All the grown-up people of the place were called together into one large house, and, in the presence of all those whose opinions were respected, each then attempted in song to lay bare his opponent's sore points. The injured man was, of course, always the challenger, and had the first right to speak. Before he began to sing at his opponent, he bound him carefully with tight bonds to the support of the house, and there he had to stand the whole evening, exposed to the mockery of the singers and the onlookers. His opponent was permitted to make use of every imaginable means of exciting him to anger; he was allowed to spit in his face, to fill his mouth with blubber, till he could not draw his breath, and, while flinging at him the most virulent abuse he could think of, was supposed to jump at him, and, with his forehead, strike him frightful "skull-breakers," wherever on his face he liked. These blows did not cease till the opponent's face was so swollen that "the cheeks were on a level with the forehead, and the eyes were closed."

And while this was going on, the bound man must not, by word or look, betray that the singer's scorn or ill-treatment made the slightest impression on him. On the contrary, a superior smile must play upon his lips, and his face must express compassion for his opponent's unsuccessful attempts to excite him and make him give himself away. His day came when the wounds on his face were well. Then he could take his revenge.

It was only specially strong and courageous men who could challenge each other to an insult duel of this description, which naturally demanded not only strength but unusual self-control. During the interval before a duel, men used to harden their foreheads as follows: The skull of a bearded seal would be bound fast to the post of the house, and the man would practice running his head against it, until the skin of his forehead was so hard that it no longer hurt him to do so. There were some who attained such dexterity that they could split the skull of a seal, Christian declared.[44]

Among other tribes the ordeal was not always so severe as among this particular group. Sometimes both contests were held the same evening, the friends of each man being present to encourage and support him by their presence and sympathetic responses of word and song. Crantz thus describes the same custom among the West Greenlanders.

The most remarkable circumstance is that they even decide their quarrels by a match of singing and dancing which they call the singing combat. If a Green-lander thinks himself aggrieved by another, he discovers no symptom of revengeful designs, anger, or vexation, but he composes a satirical poem, which he recites with singing and dancing, in the presence of his domestics, and particularly the female part of his family, till they know it by rote. He then, in the face of the whole country, challenges his antagonist to a satirical duel. The latter appears at the appointed place and both parties enter their lists. The complainant begins to sing his satire, dancing to the beat of the drum, and cheered by the echoing "Amna ajah" of his partizans, who join in every line, while he repeats so many ludicrous stories of which his adversary is the subject, that the auditors cannot forbear laughing. When he has finished, the respondent steps forth, and retorts the accusation, amidst the plaudits of his party, by a similar string of lampoons. The accuser renews the assaults, and is again rebuffed, and this continues till one of the competitors is weary. He who has the last word wins the trial, and obtains thenceforward a reputable name. An opportunity is here offered of telling very plain and cutting truths, but there must be no mixture of rudeness or passion. The assembled spectators decide the victory and the parties are in the future the best of friends. . . . . The drum-dances of the Greenlanders are, then, their Olympic Games, their Areopagus, their rostrum, their theater, their fair and their Forum. . . . . This contest is seldom attended by any disorderly conduct, except that a man that is well seconded sometimes carries off a woman whom he wishes to marry. It serves a higher purpose than mere diversion. It is an excellent opportunity for putting immorality to the blush, and cherishing virtuous principles, for reminding debtors of the duty of repayment, for branding false-hood . . . . and most of all for overwhelming adultery with its merited con-tempt.[9]

The next most interesting item on the list is the one named "Victory of Seasons." It is described by Boas (Baffin Land) as follows:

The crowd next divides itself into two parties, the ptarmigans (*axigirn*), those who were born in the winter, and the ducks (*aggirn*), or the children of the summer. A large rope of sealskin is stretched out. One party takes one end of it and tries with all its might to drag the opposite party over to its side. The others hold fast to the rope and try as hard to make ground for themselves. If the ptarmigans give way, the summer has won the game and fine weather may be expected to prevail through the winter. This game is played at the winter festival and is symbolic, being a part of their religious rites.[6]

We have placed a game of blind-man's-buff among the "Ordeal" games, though it does not rank with the others. In this the "blind man" strikes the person caught a heavy blow upon the cheek, when *he* becomes the "catcher," and does the same with the next person caught. It is an "Ordeal" game only in the sense of proving who can keep his temper. The typical "ordeal," however, is a trial of strength, either by wrestling, by boxing, or by hook-and-crook. In one form or another, these games are spoken of as in vogue from Labrador to Alaska. In some places the victor has the right to kill his opponent, though this is probably seldom done, except where some old feud exists.

"Courtship Plays" (column xxix) are mentioned but twice, in one case the "singing combat," already described, in the other a wrestling contest, the outcome of the contest being that the victorious suitor takes possession of the bride.

"Religious Plays" (column xxxi) are represented by the ventriloquial and legerdemain practices of the angekok or shaman, by the tug-of-war contests, which typify the victory of the seasons, by the chorus songs (in Alaska) used in the religious festivals; and we might have added— what does not appear on the chart—the festivals to the dead, to which the spirits of the dead are invited and entertained by songs, dancing, singing, feasting, etc.

One group still remains to be spoken of, namely, "Intellectual Plays" (column xxx). Map-drawing and checkers are spoken of a few times, but probably have been taught by the whites in every case. Besides these, very simple traditional and original songs, story-telling, carvings in wood bone, and ivory, and the highly developed inventive and imitative string figures of the cat's-cradle type—these are all that can be named of a more intellectual sort than the games of skill already described, and these, it will be noted, are plays, not games.

It is an almost pathetic fact, however, that about the only thing "owned," among these savage Eskimos, aside from their weapons and clothes, is the "original song." Although it is expected as a matter of course that the hunter will share with his neighbor the last mouthful of the game he has brought down, without expecting thanks, he who invents a new *song* is looked upon as a *benefactor*, deserving of the thanks of all.   He is the true philanthropist—"*the giver*."[44]

One general observation upon the Eskimo chart is of great interest. The East Greenlanders are supposed to be the most primitive of the Eskimo tribes, the Eskimos of Alaska the most cultured.   All of them unless it be the East Greenland group, concerning which we have found no statement regarding this particular point, give evidence both in their features and in their mythology of having some time been in contact with the Indians, a more highly developed people than the Eskimos.   All of the native gambling games may have been borrowed from the Indians, as cards, checkers, and dominoes certainly have been from the whites.   But the influence of both whites and Indians upon the Eskimos of Western Alaska, where there has been not only contact but intermarriage, has been very great, and *here* we find that the games take on a considerably more complex type, so much so as to form a marked contrast to those of the eastern Eskimos or even to those of Point Barrow.   Here again we have another indication *that complexity of games is an indication or rather an accompaniment of complexity of culture*.   As an illustration of this fact, we may note that most of the "Double Group" plays are found either in civilized Danish Greenland or in Alaska.   The two games which have been placed in the "Organized" column are both from Alaska.   "Group Competition" is much more evident in Alaska than in any other place.   "Gambling Games" are more frequent in Alaska and the Hudson Bay territory which has been so frequently visited by fishing fleets and fur traders.   The "Religious Games" are much more highly developed in Alaska, and many customs appear here as, for example, finger masks, and organized group dances, which are entirely unknown among the Eskimos outside of Alaska.   More elaboration is also found in chorus singing, mimetic dances, and festivals, and especially is this true of carvings.

CONCLUSION

Comparing, now, the results of the study of Eskimo play with that of the other four groups, we reach the following conclusions:

Somatic characteristics.—Play involving both the general and specialized use of muscles has a much larger place in the life of the Eskimo, both in amount and variety, than with any of the other groups studied, with the possible exception of the Bushmen, indicating, as we believe, a higher and more complex type of physical and mental development on the part of the Eskimos.

Organization.—(1) In the organization of their plays, the Eskimos have more "individual" plays than any of the other groups, but they also have the more complex *games* belonging to the homogeneous group, both single and double. They also have simple games of the *organized* type, which the others do not appear to have.

(2) In all five groups, unorganized play predominates over organized games.

Psychological characteristics.—(1) In all five tribes the sensory elements are very marked characteristics of the play.

(2) Rhythm is also a marked characteristic.

(3) In all the tribes except the Veddahs perception is very strongly developed, as shown in all the mimetic and dramatic entertainments. With the Veddahs the only perceptual play of which we have any account is the arrow dance, which we have *assumed* to be mimetic.

(4) The typical "games of skill" seem to be entirely lacking among the adult Veddahs, are almost wholly so among the Central Australians, were somewhat developed among the Yahgans, more so among the Bushmen, and are comparatively well developed among the Eskimos.*

(5) Games of skill are really games of judgment based upon concrete conditions; hence, the comparison made under (4) with respect to games would hold also with respect to the "practical judgment," so far as it relates to play.

(6) Games of judgment based upon *abstract* conditions find their highest representatives in courtship games, the ordeals, and religious games. It will be noticed that with these people, the last-named games are not mere play, they are real and serious attempts to reason out the ways and means of meeting real and serious situations, and the same may originally have been true of the gambling games.

* It must not be forgotten that we have much more accurate knowledge of the Eskimos than we have of the other tribes, yet with respect to general tendencies we believe the results here reached are substantially correct.

III

ANALYSIS OF PLAYS OF CIVILIZED CHILDREN

We have next to consider the play of civilized children, and in order to get the study upon a basis which will allow of legitimate comparison with that of savages, the same graphic method of analysis of individual games was adopted, and the same rubrics used throughout except in case of a few minor subdivisions where the former headings did not at all apply to modern games.

General

Chart II, while by no means covering the whole range of children's play activities, is believed to be happily representative. Mr. Chase's study[8] was based chiefly upon personal observation of the children themselves, while at play in the streets of New York City. It does not include house games. Mr. Culin's admirable study[12] upon games of Brooklyn children is also based upon personal observation (with the exception of the Philadelphia gangs) aided by the personal observation and experience of a ten-year-old boy friend. Naturally the emphasis is thrown upon *boys'* games, excluding, as it does, house games and all those played by girls alone.

Mr. Babcock's study on "Games of Washington Children"[2] seems to place more emphasis upon girls' play and that of young children, inasmuch as the various ball games and contests of strength, which are much more popular with older boys, are treated with great brevity, while the ring games have great prominence. House games are also excluded, for the most part.

Mr. McGhee's study,[34] on the other hand, gives a great number of "parlor games," as well as of outdoor plays, thus including the typical "girls' games," while Mr. Crosswell's study[10] (a portion only of which is here used) names the *favorite* games of boys *and* of girls, and includes both house and outdoor sports. It seems, therefore, that we may safely trust the conclusions reached, allowing some margin for errors of analysis, although even that has been done with as great care as the descriptions of the various authors, and the help of a Cyclopedia of Games and Sports would permit.[7a] It should be said, however, that very few plays of children below school age (six years) appear in any of these studies.

It may be needful also to offer a word of apology for the insertion of Mr. Culin's list of gangs, but it is certainly the play spirit which animates them, and they serve to bring out an interesting comparison between civilized and savage play. The same might be said of many kinds of juvenile societies. These, however, do not appear on the chart.

Accepting the chart games, then, as offering a fair "sample" of the entire general list, one rather interesting comparison at once appears, respecting the difference between the sexes in choice of games. That portion of the chart in which boys' games predominate (Mr. Culin's) is characterized by continuous lines of entries, and fewer of them. They are expanded vertically, while in the portions including games of both boys and girls in about equal numbers the lines are more broken and straggling, that is, they are expanded horizontally. This difference is of course due to the presence of the girls' games, and it bears out the opinion which several authors have expressed, namely, that boys play fewer games than girls, and have much stronger preferences for those which are their favorites.

We question, however, the further statement of these same authors who observe that males show greater variability than females in choice of games. Our chart suggests that the difference in variation is a difference in *kind*, not in degree—that, given an equal amount of energy to both the boy and the girl, the first will expend it upon a few lines of interest while the second will divide it up among many. We may say, perhaps, that the variation of boys is up and down the scale, that is, vertically, while girls vary in the direction of the "all-round" interest, that is, horizontally. If this be true, and granting, also, that play is typical of life in general, we should expect to find among men a relatively larger number representing both the highest and lowest in race development, while a relatively larger number of women should represent the "many sided," the humanitarian interests. Whether the first part of this proposition be true or not, namely that more men than women vary *above* the average, cannot be known experimentally until women are free as men to live out their highest capacities, unhindered by a wage so small as to debar them from advantages which men find necessary for their best achievement, and untrammeled by fear of intrigue and treachery from which they have, as yet, no means of protection, except by withdrawal from the danger, and likewise from their opportunity also. But the other end of the argument, namely, that more males than females vary *below* the average, finds some confirmation in the fact that, both in London and in New York, presumably representative cities, about two-thirds of the defective children are males.* On the other hand, when we consider that the highly organized games and city gangs, representing a very objective and a very intense life, are more typical of boys, while societies for mere play,

* See an article by the author in *Pedagogical Seminary*[25] (March, 1907), 31.

self-improvement, benevolent and altruistic organizations of all sorts, that is, interests of a more subjective type, appeal far more strongly to girls than to boys, we find still further confirmation of this possible law of variation.   It explains, also, why girls can be much more easily diverted from one interest to another.   They have, if we may trust the charts, more inherent tendencies with which to respond to various sorts of stimulation.   This is in line with Mendel's discovery that, physiologically, the female is more complex even in the original cell.[5a]   On the other hand, the very fact of fewer interests on the part of boys, i.e., fewer avenues for escape of nervous energy, accounts in itself, perhaps, for the greater intensity.

Another comparison also suggests itself here, namely, that the difference between civilization and non-civilization may consist simply in an exaggeration and combination of both these types of variation.   Variation *up and down* the scale certainly seems to appear in the superior intellectual capacity of at least a few among civilized individuals, while there is certainly a far larger proportion of imbeciles and defectives among civilized than among savage peoples.   On the other hand, no one would question for a moment that the *range* of interests is far *broader* among the civilized races.

Comparative.—The details of the children's chart may be considered somewhat briefly, inasmuch as the more careful analysis of the chart of Eskimo play has already called attention to significant points. The group of columns v–ix under "Somatic Characteristics" teaches beyond all question, that if children are let alone to find amusement and self-training as impulse directs, by far the greater part of their pleasure will be found in reactions which involve the activity of the whole body.   Many of the house games, even, involve frequent change of position, or marching, or perhaps a scramble for seats.   In fact the column indicating activity of the whole body is more continuous with the children than it is with the Eskimos.   Furthermore, the proportion of "Running Games" is far greater with the children.

If we turn over the "Fighting Plays" (column vi), arm-tracking, hook-and-crook, foot-pushing, etc., to the "Whole Body" plays (see p. 26), as was done with the Eskimo lists, there is again left a collection of games requiring more specialized muscular control.   The list includes marbles, juggling, tossed ball, jackstraws, pease-porridge-hot, missy-massy, two little blackbirds, "this is the church," cat's-cradle, up-Jenks, parlor croquet, parchesi, bean bags, Simon says "thumbs up," ring on the string, pillow dex, tit-tat-taw, mumblety-peg, roller skates, bicycling.   So far as the employment of skill is concerned, the Eskimo games stand well in comparison;

however, drawing, painting, and playing on musical instruments do not happen to be represented on the chart of children's plays.

"Quiet Plays" are about equally well represented on both charts, with this difference, however, that on the Eskimo chart a larger place proportionately is given to singing, dancing, and drumming, i.e., to rhythmic plays. Dancing is not once mentioned on the children's chart as a play for its own sake, but it is often an accessory to other plays and games. Some of the quiet plays are included in the list just given; others are, hunt the button, picture-tossing (a gambling game), some singing games, Quaker meeting, post-office, wishing rhymes, rhymes of augury, jingles of various types, "this little pig went to market," "dog Latin," "cat Latin" (i.e., plays of the vocal organs), hide the button, various guessing games, a great variety of card games, dolls, forfeits, dramatic plays, parchesi, and many similar games, charades, riddles, puzzles, checkers, proverbs, philopena, consequences, "cross-questions and crooked answers," "table rappings," chess, twenty questions, backgammon, dominoes, reading, making pictures, telling stories, making toys, etc.

Unlike the muscular games, into which the Eskimos seem to bring relatively a greater amount of skill than the children, the "Quiet Games" on the children's chart more often call for quick perception or imagination or constructive powers, as, for example, acting charades, guessing riddles, conundrums, etc.

Under the second general rubric, "Organization," proportionally fewer "Individual" games appeared as compared with the Eskimo chart. The

Type of Organization reason of this is undoubtedly found in the exclusion of most of the games of children under six years of age (school age).

Among those which do appear, however, are bonfires, rope-jumping, hop-scotch (which is sometimes played alone, sometimes with others), a pretty little finger play in which the child places the hands back to back, then closes them over the fingers, with the exception of the upward-pointing index fingers, while she repeats the words

> This is the church,
> And this is the steeple;
> Open the door,
> And see all the people.

Tops, "buzz," and cat's-cradle, coasting, skates, roller skates, dolls, housekeeping, swimming, swinging, kites, puzzles, jackstraws, jackstones, play wagon, bicycling, kites, reading, fishing, boat-sailing, roll hoop, cars, "making things" appear. It may be noticed, however, that while the number of individual plays is smaller than with the Eskimos, the variety is much greater. But while on the Eskimo chart the list of "Individual Plays" and those of the "Undefined Group" were in about equal proportions, on the children's chart the entries under "Undefined Group" greatly exceeded the others. This again was partly due to exclusion of plays of the youngest children, but the results of columns xiv, xv, and xvi lead one to feel that it was partly due also to a greater tendency to organization in American children. The plays represented by "Single Pair," "Double Group," and "Organized Group" are all better represented on the children's chart, and what is of still greater interest, two classes of games were noted on the children's chart, namely, "Team Games," and "Gangs," which had nothing corresponding to them on the chart of the Eskimos.

Again the same difference between unorganized and organized play appeared in columns xvii and xviii, where the proportion of games to play was much greater on the children's chart. We can hardly resist the conclusion suggested by the double study, that organization is much more typical of children's play in civilized countries than among adult savages. This opinion would be much further strengthened had "societies" been included in the chart, as well as gangs. Furthermore, in both of these, as well as in the team games, a new and additional element of organization appeared, namely, organization for permanency.

A comparative study of the psychical characteristics showed that sensation had a slightly more emphatic place on the Eskimo chart (column Psychological xix). The same was true of "Rhythmic Plays" (column Character- xx). But here again we miss the plays of the children under istics school age, who were, therefore, too young to be playing on the streets.

"Dramatic" tendencies (column xxi), i.e., perceptual play, were about equally represented on both charts, and probably deserved on both a stronger representation than they had.

In "Games of Skill" (column xxii), the Eskimos certainly seemed to be relatively in advance of the children. This does not mean that they have more games of that character, but that a larger proportion of what they have are of that type. Like the children, Eskimos voluntarily place themselves under a rigorous course of self-training.

The sense of the ludicrous (column xxiii), while strong with the Eskimos, appeared to be even stronger with the children. Playing practical jokes seems to be one of the strongest incentives in the formation of street gangs. Among other plays mentioned are leapfrog and several similar games; last tag, in which a ridiculing couplet is hurled at the one who happens to be last in reaching his retreat; "follow your leader," who tries to conduct his party through all the absurd and difficult feats possible; Spanish fly, similar to the last in type; several plays, the purpose of which is to foist some practical joke on a new-comer in the neighborhood; snap the whip, mouse trap, contemptuous rhymes, April-fool tricks (not shown on the chart), "dog Latin," "cat Latin," "smiling angel," "pretty maids," and other games, in which one who makes a wrong guess is derided in some way; "Buffalo Bill" and other "shows"; battle, knucks, stagecoach, and similar games involving a series of ridiculous motions; forfeits, acting charades, Simon says "thumbs up," philopena, roly-poly, cross-questions, Quaker meeting, etc.

"Individual Competition" (column xxiv) was a very strong characteristic on both charts, but "Group Competition" had a very much more prominent place on the children's chart. This study confirmed the conclusions reached under the rubric, "Type of Organization."

The children had a much larger variety of "Games of Chance" (column xxvi) other than gambling games. Many of these were card games, but among those which were not were "splitting tops," prophets, Hallowe'en charms, wishing rhymes, several guessing games, dominoes, parchesi, consequences, "cross-questions and crooked answers," and "counting out" to see who shall be "it."

The study of "Gambling Games" (column xxvii) showed that while Eskimos are winning stakes with dice, roulette, archery, and throwing games, American children are winning them with marbles, buttons, pennies, pictures, eggs, cards, and other devices.

The "Ordeal" (column xxviii) would seem, perhaps, to belong exclusively to savage society, but apparently it has its counterpart in the play of civilized children and youth. It is a marked characteristic of many of the city gangs. Our national game, baseball, may be considered to have in it the element of "ordeal," in somewhat the same sense as the "singing contests" of the Eskimos, inasmuch as it demands the same perfect self-control on the part of the players. It is our belief that the young men who excel in this game so regard it, and that this feeling of being "on trial," in a sense which makes it a character test, accounts in large measure for the fascination of the game. But aside from this, most of the city gangs impose some sort of ordeal upon the incoming members, while younger boys not formally organized into gangs have various ceremonies of "bumping," stuffing the new boy's mouth with straw or earth, soiling his clothes with tar, and jokes of a similar nature.[12]

"Courtship Plays" (column xxix) were far more numerous on the children's chart, but with this difference, that with the *little* children, at least, they are mere play with almost no meaning. Rhythm, song, and motion are the really attractive elements in them. The unmeaning jumble of words, which Mr. Babcock found in use in many of the games played by Washington children, showed that the players were scarcely thinking of what the rhymes meant. With the Eskimo, however, the case is quite different. To him a courtship game is the "real thing." With the ending of his singing contest or wrestling match he wins or looses a bride.

The same is true of "Religious Plays" (column xxxi). With civilized children it is a question if any very deep religious fervor pervades their plays of "funeral," "Quaker meeting," and spirit communications by "table rappings." With the Eskimos, it is no make-believe when the spirits of departed friends are invited to share in the songs, dancing, and festivities for the dead. The dead are present; they listen to the songs composed for them; they partake of the food, and when the festivities are over, they are given specific instructions to go back to their home in the earth, or sea, or wherever it may be.

The column "Intellectual Play" (column xxx) furnished one of the most interesting comparisons of the whole study. On the Eskimo chart we found the following games and plays: original songs, story-telling, carvings, checkers (introduced, and not in general use) map-drawing (suggested in every case, probably, by foreigners), singing contests (in which the main purpose is psychical), and angakok or shaman performances (in which there is not only a psychical *motif* but often a considerable amount of legerdemain).

On the children's chart, too, are stories, also reading and "making things," which corresponds somewhat to the inventiveness shown in the Eskimo carvings, toys, and maps. Then we found several types of intellectual play not represented on the Eskimo chart. Some of these are of a very low grade intellectually, mostly played by young children—such as the guessing games of buttons, "this and that," hide the thimble, birds, ribbons, "pretty maids," good night, etc., in which the intellectual play is merely a guess, without any basis of judgment. But there are other guessing games which involve more intellectuality. "Hull gull" trains in counting, and also has the element of competition. Object-guessing, guided by questions and answers, involves the "abstract judgment." The same is true of "twenty questions." Then there is the group of games represented by checkers, backgammon, and chess, and the card games represented by authors. Simon says "thumbs up" is a motor-auditory play; Jacob and Ruth and shouting proverbs are auditory plays; philopena, a memory play; cross-questions and crooked answers, forfeits, and consequences are humorous plays. Then came those of a still more purely intellectual nature, such as charades, puzzles, rebuses, etc. All these made a list of quite a different character from those found on the Eskimo chart. With the Eskimos the best intellectual element was found in *play*. With the children it was found in *both play and games*.

IV

GENERAL COMPARISON OF THE TWO FIVEFOLD GROUPS WITH RESPECT TO PLAY CHARACTERISTICS

On the whole, then, it must be said, that:

1. Comparing chart with chart, the play of the savage tribes studied and the play of civilized children *do not run in parallel lines.* All the elements which appear in savage play reappear in that of civilized children, but in some respects the resemblances are very striking, while in others the differences are very great.

Two Fivefold Groups

2. Furthermore, this difference is not only one of proportions in the elements involved, but there is also a difference in quantity and kind, both the number and variety of games being comparatively very much greater among the children. In fact, Mr. Crosswell states that his reports from the public-school children alone named over five hundred different amusements.[10]

With the Eskimos there is a marked repetition of the same plays in the accounts of different authors, even where the observations were many hundred miles apart and among groups which have no communication with each other. The children's chart, although including one and one-half times as many plays as the Eskimo chart, and although the same method of recording has been employed, shows far less repetition.

3. There is also a difference in complexity. This complexity is most clearly shown in the charts, in columns xv, xvi, xviii, xxv, and xxx, but it is still more evident in the *process of analysis* of the games, the children's games being far more difficult to separate into elements and to redistribute into a true classification of characteristics. In fact, the work was done over and over many times before a classification was found which seemed satisfactory.

4. Further, a new element disclosed itself in children's play, with the appearance of "teams," "gangs," and "societies," namely, organization of the group into *permanent relations* for purposes of play. We find nothing whatever of this in any of the five tribes studied. The nearest approach to it is among the Central Australians, where certain groups have certain totemic ceremonies belonging to and played by that group alone. But the difference between the two is this: among the Australians the group exists

because of the totemic ancestry, and independently of their dramatic ceremonial plays, *not for the sake of the plays*, while with children the "team" and "gang" and many of the "societies" exist merely for the sake of augmenting the pleasure and efficiency of the participants, and the accomplishment of more difficult results.   Such organizations foster a long-sustained interest and the pursuit of distant ends.

5. Play among savages is far less dissociated from the serious occupations of life than is the case with children, except with little children.   In the ordeal and religious plays, the singing contests, and in the festivals to the dead, and less truly, perhaps, in the gambling games, there is no dissociation at all.   The play is the logical expression of their philosophy of living.   And even the mimetic plays and dances, and the ceremonials of the Australians are not something invented for play's sake, but a faithful reproduction in pantomime of what they themselves have experienced, or what they believe their ancestors have experienced.   So markedly true to this dramatic type form is the play of the groups here studied, that we are inclined to believe that all play in its primitive forms had its genesis in actual experience, and that it is only when the experience is forgotten, or is crystallized into a myth, that it gradually becomes conventionalized and handed down by one generation to another as a "traditional" game.   This theory furnishes, possibly, an additional explanation (see p. 13) of why a people so isolated as the Veddahs or Central Australians should have such a paucity of games. The conditions under which they are living are so similar to those of their ancestors, that their play is still permeated with all the associations which it originally possessed, and their monotonous lives suggest no new associations.   Hence their play still retains its dramatic form.   The Bushmen and Yahgans, on the contrary, driven from one part of the continent to another by the stronger tribes which pressed upon them, have had a more varied history; so, while retaining the *activity* of the play as an agreeable exercise, they have, in some cases, lost the particular associations originally surrounding the imitative sport, and, keeping the form only, have developed it, meanwhile, into a "game of skill."

The same process of dissociation of thought, through change of habitat, has undoubtedly taken place with the Eskimos, though in a time long past. But with them the long months of Arctic night, almost compelling them to *play or die*, have nurtured the play instinct, and developed it far beyond that of similar savage tribes not thus thrown back upon their own resources for means with which to pass away the tedious hours while shut in by darkness or storm.

In confirmation of the theory that games as well as play originated in experience, we are fortunately able to quote from Rasmussen[44] a description of an Eskimo game *in process of making*. He says:

I stood in the center of a gay group, on just such a late summer evening; the men, old and young, sat clustered round a seal-catcher who was making a sledge. Behind us shouting children played their games.

Suddenly one of them called out, *qaqaitsorssuakut!* which, in this connection, means, "The men with boats without masts!"

The cry was echoed by the whole tribe of them, and they tore in a wild race up to the hills, where they hid in the hollows of the stones.

I wanted to know what it all meant, and my question gave one of the old ones an opportunity of narrating an interesting legend.

"Do you see that low, black iceberg yonder?" he began; "that is what the children are running away from. In olden days, at the approach of the first dark evenings, there was always a good lookout kept on the sea, for it sometimes happened that ships came into sight, out at sea, ships without masts. They were *nakasungnaitsut*, the short-legged men, or, as they were also called, *qavdlunatsait*, a race of white men who were very warlike; they used to come up here with great boats, the sterns of which were higher than the bows, so the old people tell us.

"These white men came originally from these parts, so tradition relates in the legend of the girl who married a dog. These *qavdlunatsait* were amongst her children; when they grew up, she made a boat out of a sole of a leather boot and started them out to sea, so that they might sail to the country where the white men lived.

"'Ye shall be fighting men!' she had said to them when they went away. These are the words of the legend.

"After that, men were always afraid of the ships that came up here, for they invariably picked quarrels and killed. But often a dark iceberg was mistaken for them, and roused false terror in the village; and that is what is now grown into a game among the children.

"One year it was already winter when sledges, which were out hunting walruses, discovered one of the white men's big ships frozen up in the ice. That was out beyond Northumberland Island. The people knew from experience that sooner or later these men would come and attack them, so they decided to be beforehand with them.

"Armed with lances and harpoons they rushed up against them on foot. The ice round the ship was new and smooth, and so they bound the skin from the palate of seals round their feet, that they might not slip. The white men were taken by surprise, and, as they found it difficult to run on the smooth ice, it was an easy matter to overcome them. Thus the men from these parts avenged the deaths of their compatriots."

With the above account of the way in which Eskimo children play, compare the following accounts given by Mr. Babcock in "Games of Washington children."[2]

A mother having children for all the days of the week cautions Sunday, the eldest, to "take care of Monday and all the rest and don't let them get hurt. If you do you know what I'll give you." After the mother has gone the witch comes in and says: "Little girl, please go (pointing) and get me a match for my pipe. There's a bulldog over there and I am afraid to go." She goes for the match. He snatches up Monday and makes off. The mother returns.

Mother: "Where is my Monday gone?"

Sunday: "The old witch has got her."

Mother: "Do you know what I told you? I'm going to beat you."

She makes a pretense of doing so. This program is repeated until all the children are stolen except Sunday. At the next visit the witch says, "Little girl, little girl, come with me and I'll give you some candy." She goes with him. All the children are shut up in a room. During the absence of the witch the mother breaks into it and rescues them.

The second play is equally suggestive.

Witch discovered making a fire. Enter mother with children behind her in single file, each grasping the clothes of the one next in front. This line marches around singing,

> Chickamy, chickamy, cramery, crow,
> I went to the well to wash my toe,
> When I came back my chicken was gone.

Pausing before the fire-builder, the mother asks, in continuation of the song, "What time is it, old witch?" The witch replies, "One o'clock." The march and song are resumed. On coming around again, the question is repeated, and the answer is, "Two o'clock." This is continued with ascending numerals, until the twelfth round. After the answer "Twelve o'clock," this conversation begins:

Mother: "What are you doing there?"

Witch: "Making a fire."

Mother: "What are you making a fire for?"

Witch: "To roast chickens."

Mother: "Whose chickens?"

Witch (fiercely): "Those of your flock."

She springs out at them and they scatter. . . . . On the eastern shore of Maryland the mother fights for the chickens.[2]

6. With the phylogenetic group there seems to be less differentiation between the sexes in their choice of games than with American youth. We have found no account of women joining in the wrestling games or any of the plays which are intended merely as feats of strength, but they play baseball, tag, chase, leapfrog, etc., even with little babies in their hoods, with quite as much zest as do the men.[60]

7. Lastly, sensation, perception, and judgment, *when applied to actual concrete conditions*, find ample exercise among the five savage tribes, in

both play and games (see p. 41).   The abstract or philosophical judgment and the reasoning powers find partial expression in ordeal, courtship, and religious plays and in their festivals, and, frequently, in the mimetic dances and dramatic ceremonies, but not one native *game* has been discovered in any of our researches relating to these particular tribes, in which the chief source of enjoyment consisted in purely intellectual activity, such as, for example, riddles.

V

STUDY OF CHILDREN'S PLAY BY PERIODS

Thus far we have failed to find a complete parallelism between our phylogenetic and ontogenetic groups. Shall we then leave the subject with these general comparisons, or shall we attempt still further to determine whether there be *any* ground for the theory that the child recapitulates the experience of the race? The latter seems the more inviting course to pursue. The discussion of a theory is sometimes more helpful than the theory itself, and frequently leads the participants to build better than they know by revealing to them that the theory under contention is, after all, but a partial statement of a far grander, richer, and more fundamental truth than they have yet discovered.

Periods of Development

In the more detailed comparison which follows, of the play of savages and of children's play, *the attempt will be made to discover whether the play of savages corresponds to any part of children's play, to any particular type, or to any particular period of ontogenetic development.*

In order to accomplish this task, it will not only be necessary to discover the various *elements* which enter into play—an analysis already performed—but *the particular elements which characterize different periods* of a child's development must also be determined. In this part of the investigation we shall depend almost wholly upon data already available through the researches of others, notably Dr. G. Stanley Hall, Professor Barnes, Messrs. Gulick, Crosswell, Babcock, Lindly, Sheldon, France, Monroe, Culin, Kirkpatrick, Miss Freer, Miss Shinn, and others (see bibliography). While thus scanning the life of the individual purely as a matter of convenience, in treating the subject by periods we must be guarded at every point against any thought of abrupt transition from one period to another. There is no exact moment when any individual passes from infancy to childhood, or from childhood to youth, nor is there any law which applies, without variation, to any individual. Nevertheless there is a certain advantage in isolating one period from another, in order to bring out its striking characteristics, and to get a basis of comparison not otherwise obtainable. Such a method, artificial though it be, is helpful in grasping relationships and in determining sequences, if any are to be found, in the developing powers of mind and body.

In order to make the exact nature of the problem explicit, it will be necessary to summarize somewhat carefully the conclusions already reached on the ontogenetic side. In so doing we shall quote freely from the above-named authors, adopting, for convenience, the classification into periods, as made by Gulick,[23] namely, (1) babyhood, approximately from birth to three; (2) early childhood, from the beginning of the third year to the seventh; (3) later childhood, from the beginning of the seventh year to the twelfth, (4) early adolescence, from the beginning of the twelfth to the seventeenth year; (5) later adolescence, from the beginning of the seventeenth year to the twenty-third. We will study separately the characteristics of each of these five periods.

What are the plays of childhood and youth? [says Gulick]. Do they form a logical and coherent whole? Is there any orderly progression? If so, whence do they start, and to what do they lead? . . . . Hard and fast divisions [into periods] cannot be made, not only because they do not exist, but because children vary so much—some are precocious, others are slow. All that is attempted is to have years in which it is possible to recognize certain great groups of activities. In this classification it must be remembered that each group includes all the preceding. The individual loses nothing as he grows. Everything that he has acquired remains to him as a joy and a recreation, if it is in the right relations. The baby will play in the sand for hours, making marks with his fingers, picking up a handful and letting it trickle out. Such simple plays as these never lose their interest.

But we do find new interests coming in as the child advances in life, and *these new interests* are the elements which differentiate one period of development from another. In order to get a clear understanding of this *genetic* or *transitional* aspect of the play activities, it will be advisable to study the above-named periods from three distinct points of view, namely: (1) the objective or factual standpoint; (2) the subjective or psychological standpoint; (3) the biological standpoint.

FIRST PERIOD—FROM BIRTH TO BEGINNING OF THIRD YEAR

"How do babies play?" asks Gulick, and answers the question thus:

All will recognize . . . . the characteristics of . . . . plays of babyhood . . . . the spontaneous kicking . . . . the clasping movements, the movements of the head. . . . . The baby rapidly progresses to playing in **Factual Phase of Play** more complicated ways . . . . to pick things up and drop them, to play with sand . . . . piling it up and digging in it with the fingers, scooping it with the hand, digging it with a stick, sticking little sticks in it, covering things up with sand, and . . . . making little imitations of things. He soon loves to play with blocks, pieces of wood, sticks, straws, anything out of which he can construct something. He will take delight in running and throwing his arms at the same time. Throwing . . . . a ball engages his passionate interest.[23]

We might add to these plays the peek-a-boo games which babies delight in, the stair-climbing, pounding on the piano, hiding behind chairs, the sensori-motor "little-pig-went-to-market" jingle, and in the latter part of the period, the pleasure in listening to nursery rhymes having a very marked rhythm, especially when accompanied by rhythmic action.

Meanwhile, what is going on in the baby's mind? So far as we know, the infant's first consciousness is an aggregation of sensations unassociated in consciousness with each other, and appearing gradually in his psychical world, but bringing with them, neverthe-less, affective characteristics of pleasantness and unpleasant-ness.[51] As the senses become acute and the muscles more responsive to the stimulation of the nerve endings, the lifelong task of investigation is begun. The ball is pinched, pounded, tasted, the tin cup banged, the spoon dropped, the hair pulled, the face scratched—at first without purpose, but very soon from choice, in order to repeat a sensation which has once proved agreeable. When memory is sufficiently developed so that the child chooses between activities, voluntarily returning to one rather than to another, we say, "He is playing," but to the child it is not play; it is the serious work of life, in quite the same sense, probably, as that of the astronomer who forgets all else in absorption in some new discovery. Both play with balls, each after a manner characteristic of his own stage of development.

Subjective Phase

But note that the baby's absorption is in the sensation and in the activity, not in the object for its own sake. The child builds with blocks, but he does not care to preserve what he builds; the sensory delight which comes with the crash of their downfall and the mere pleasure of doing are enough.

Note, too, that through all this period, reflex imitation is very marked. The child laughs when others laugh, cries when they cry, "weeps with those who weep," shares their anger, imitates their gestures and tone of voice— many times without volition, almost unconsciously—yet he is, nevertheless, enlarging, meanwhile, his world of sensation, and co-ordinating muscular activity therewith. Sensation, motion, emotion, and their relations to each other—these are the problems, of no small magnitude, toward which the baby mind is turned. Yet the greater part of the intellectual life seems to be an almost uncontrolled response to whatever stimuli, physical and social, happen to surround him.

In what general way may we characterize these interests, these plays? It is evident that they are progressive in regard to complexity of movement, (also) the first movements . . . . of the baby are feeble as compared to his later movements; his later movements are feeble as compared to his movements as a little boy. . . . . Then, too, we may easily see that these movements are the fundamental ones that become reflex

Biological Phase

during later life, the earlier bodily movements of the baby certainly do.   All the mechanics of running, jumping, throwing, handling tools, and the use of the body become thoroughly reflex in later life, and this is the period in which they are becoming reflex.   It is to be noted that these activities are individualistic.   They are not games; the little child does not play games. . . . . It is also evident that these earliest activities are common not only to all human races, but also to the higher animals, in varying degree. . . . . A moment's reflection on the develop- ment of the nervous system will show that we have a most intimate relation between this psychical development, and the development of the spinal cord and the brain.   Recent investigators tell us that during the first one or two or three years of life, the spinal cord, together with certain lower parts of the brain, comes into almost complete activity; that it is the period for the acquirement of all those activities that depend upon the spinal cord.   These, as we all know, are the reflex activities.   They constitute activities dependent upon the "lower level," so called, of the development of the nervous system, according to the Hughlings Jackson theory.[23]

SECOND PERIOD—BEGINNING OF THIRD YEAR TO THE SEVENTH

During early childhood—three to seven—children enjoy building with blocks. At first the buildings are simple and regular, the blocks stood up in rows more or less distant.   The idea of regularity appears to be definite,
Factual Phase but [there is] little idea of symmetry until the latter part of this period and then I suspect it is the copying of older children. Children enjoy swinging, are fond of climbing, will climb low trees, will climb banisters, experiment with jumping from chairs, with jumping from steps. . . . . To cut things with scissors, or with a knife, is the basis of a whole group of activities of a play nature.   Swinging in various forms he [the child] loves to do. See-saw interests all children.   The joggling board of some of our southern states, being analogous to a large springboard, is of great interest.   Riding hobby horses, driving a broom, and a multitude of exercises of a similar nature, are common. . . . . Thus we see the boy soon learning to shoot with bow and arrow, with sling, with rubber shooter, with the protean forms of toy guns.   We observe his growing interest in work with tools. . . . . The attachment for dolls comes in the latter part of this period among girls.[23]

Fortunately, we have a supplementary study upon children between five and six years of age, of so great value that we quote at length.   Miss Sisson,[53] writing of the free play of her kindergarten children before school, at recess, and at noon, states that they "divided themselves into four distinct groups, though sometimes a play of more than unusual interest would unite them all."   Concerning their spontaneous choice of play activities, she writes:

The first group consisted of the older and more active boys.   Their plays required much action.   They ran, they wrestled, they climbed with all the might that was in them. They played a great many highly imaginative games, some of them rather rough and boisterous. During the time that I observed them, not quite two months, I noticed thirty-one distinct kinds of spontaneous, dramatic plays, in which almost all this class of children were engaged; for instance, policeman, hunter, store, electric-light men, etc. . . . .

The next group consisted of older girls and some of the little ones, whom they drew in to play minor parts. Their games were almost entirely dramatic, and consisted usually of playing house or playing school. These plays were generally conducted very quietly, out on the sand pile at first, where they built the houses, gardens, etc., and then when it became rainy, in the hat room or in the woodshed. . . . .

The third group was made up of the smaller children, and one of the older but more bashful girls. They generally indulged in simple representative games, but spent a large portion of their time running from one part of the yard to another, because of some passing whim, over to the faucet to get a drink, or over to the sand pile to see what the others were doing. . . . .

The last group was a miscellaneous remainder. . . . . They had no leader, for they were not organized. . . . . The chief attraction to this group was the swing. They very seldom ran. . . . .

The duration of a game varied greatly; sometimes it would last but a minute or two. Once such a play as the "wild hog" occupied the attention of the larger boys for two and one-half days. Again they had a slanting beam, on which the boys played for nearly the whole time for nearly a week. One boy pounded a bolt steadily for nearly twenty minutes; he played that he was mending a car, and said that he was playing that the bolt was a screw, that he needed a screw-driver, but as he had only a hammer, he should have to pound with it. He stopped only when the bell rang.

An important point to notice is the appearance of the same play on consecutive days. The swing has been in use all the time with trifling interruptions, from the time it was put up in September. They slid and performed on the beam, one end of which was on the fence, and the other on the ground, every day for a month, but at the end of that time, it was accidentally thrown down. . . . . Hunting either wild hogs or other animals appeared thirteen times during about thirty-five days. Tops were on hand every day, from October twenty-sixth, till about the first of December. There were but three or four days, during the last two months of the term, that the girls did not play either house or school. The following list of plays of the larger boys will show the order in which these plays occurred, and the frequency with which they took place: October twenty-fourth, Policeman; twenty-fifth, Policeman and hunters; twenty-sixth, Wild Horses, Hunters, and Salvation Army; thirtieth, Butcher and House; November first, Butcher, Jail; second, Hunting, Cars, Circus; third, Butcher, Band, Procession; sixth, Band, Ladder, Steamer, and Circus; seventh, Ladder, played with as Steam-engine, and Circus-train; eighth, Ladder, played with as Pipe-organ, and then Wood-saw; ninth, with ladder as a steamer; thirteenth, Dragon; fourteenth, Wild Hog; sixteenth, Wild Hog, Train, Indians; seventeenth, Wild Hog, Indians; twentieth, Merry-go-Round; twenty-first, Cars; twenty-second, Circus and Menagerie; twenty-third, Policeman; twenty-fourth, Cars; twenty-eighth, Horse; December fifth, Electric Light Men, Circus; seventh, Wild Horse, Bear, Robbers, and Policeman, Electric Launch, Steamer and Boats, Indians; eighth, Indians; eleventh, Santa Claus, Wild Horse, Store, Street-watering Cars; twelfth, Teams of Horses, Telephone.

The general quality in the plays that attracted and held the children was action, found either in purely physical plays or dramatic plays in which all could take part. And in their representative plays, those that dealt with natural objects had a greater holding power than those that dealt with artificial things.

As you will have noticed, the traditional games, such as "London Bridge" and "Prisoner's Base" played but little part in the amusement of kindergarten children. Out of doors, the game of "Hide and Seek" was the only organized traditional play that was suggested by the children. Near the beginning of the term, I showed them how to play "Drop the Handkerchief." They enjoyed it then, but did not call for it themselves. Sometimes their dramatic play came to have a set form, but that set form was always at the mercy of the leader, who varied it to suit himself. . . . . Though the children are still very imitative, they seemed to have developed a good deal of originality, and independence. For instance, when they were standing on the ring in the kindergarten, ready for their games, I asked the musician to play an unfamiliar tune, and told the children to do anything they liked as long as the music continued. These are the answers the children gave me as to what they did, the last time we did this: "Hopped," "crawled as a horse," "elephant," "grasshopper," "black-legged man," "bird," "scare-crow," "bear," "river," "sand-bug," "wheel." You will notice that but two played the same thing. You will notice that but one confined himself to the purely physical desire for motion, all the others being representative. . . . . Only the older children were present when this observation was made.

The plays seemed to come from two entirely different sources. The first was the compelling power of the leader. A child obliged the other boys, by means of his personal influence, to make the ladder a wood-saw, when they wanted it to be a steamer. He could almost always draw the boys of his group into the play he wanted. Second, the special novelty or interest in the play itself led to its choice, even when not forced upon the attention of the school by an aggressive child. Thus the boys were greatly delighted with the idea of becoming acrobats, and without any incentive but the pleasure of the act itself each boy tried for days to equal the feats of Lewis, a quiet, non-aggressive boy.

Both these classes of play were suggested by the environment of the children. Every public event which they saw in the world around them, or heard talked about by grown people, was mirrored in their play. But whatever they did, or from whatever reason they did it, their whole hearts went into their play. It was an expression of the children themselves, and a truer one than any set exercise or experiment could give.

Now, what are the subjective or psychological characteristics of these plays? Sensation still affords great delight to the child, but rhythmic motions, sounds, and plays—the characteristic of which is to reinforce the effect of isolated sensations—are eagerly sought. Sensori-motor plays still have a strong hold upon the child, but they are enjoyed not merely for the sake of the sensation or action, but sensation and action now have definite meaning. The child "emerges into a world of things, as opposed to a world of sensations." *But a world of things-implies lively perceptive and apperceptive activies* both of which are undoubtedly uppermost in all the imitative and dramatic plays which reach their climax at about the sixth or eighth year. Furthermore, the effect of the action, as well as the action itself; control of environment, as well as mere stimulation by, and reaction to, environmental influences; *manipulation* and *choice* of means to accomplish definite ends; and eager welcoming of any new experience, these enter into all the spontaneous plays. The general type is still largely instinctive and is highly imitative in character.

The child is immensely inquisitive [says Gulick] and wishes to find things out. Its play is largely influenced by this feeling. I do not think that the destructive play of boys is merely destructive. It is related to the acquisition of knowledge and of the construction of other things. . . . . Children before seven *rarely play games** spontaneously. They do so sometimes under the stimulus of older children or of adults. The same fact may be stated in regard to competition. The plays before seven are almost exclusively non-competitive.[23]

Comparing the plays of this period with those of babyhood, I would say that they are far more constructive, far greater in range, that the muscular movements involved were larger, more powerful, more sustained, but still of much the same character. Unless influenced by adults, there is but little fine work with the fingers and wrists, not very much of delicate co-ordination. The movements are the larger movements of the trunk, shoulders, and elbows. It is a time of great activity. There is but little sitting still or keeping still when awake. . . . .[32]

[Physiologically, the brain has attained nearly its full size by the seventh or eighth year; medullation in the peripheral system is almost completed in the first five years, and the limbs are growing rapidly.]

THIRD PERIOD—YEARS SEVEN TO TWELVE

We quote again from Gulick as to the games characteristic of the period seven to twelve.

* Italics mine.

The ball games are played, "one old cat," an elementary baseball game, swimming and rowing. . . . . Boys delight in the use of tools during this period, and in building all sorts of things, making little streams and dams, paddle-wheels and boats, simple machinery of all kinds.   Many games are now played, "duck on the rock," "black man," "blindman's-buff," "crockinol," "croquet," "leapfrog," simple feats of all kinds, turning somersaults, rolling over backwards, marbles, "mumble the peg," "prisoner's base," "puss in the corner," "tiddledywinks," "touchwood." . . . . Girls play some of these games, "hunt the handkerchief," many games in which the circle is used. . . . . During what I have called later childhood—from seven to twelve . . . . we have the height of . . . . housekeeping arrangements. . . . . At about ten the interest in dolls seems to wane, but taking its place is an interest in babies. . . . . Every one of our babies has been borrowed by neighbors' children of about this age. . . .   Boys do not borrow our babies. . . . , Boys want knives to whittle, all sorts of plays with strings, flying kites.[23]

Factual Phase

Mr. Stewart Culin's study on "Street Games of Boys in Brooklyn, New York"[12] has a special interest for us just here, in the fact that his information was obtained from a lad of ten years who had himself taken part in all the games.   We may be sure then that they are truly representative of the period of which we are speaking, although we might expect the emphasis to shift somewhat, from the simpler to the more complex games during the next year or two.   He gives us a list of thirty-nine games and plays, an analysis of which has been made in the children's chart, under Mr. Culin's name.   The "gangs" apparently belong to an older period, as Mr. Culin's informant knew very little about them, or it may be that they are becoming less popular than formerly, as other sources of enjoyment become available.

During these years from seven to twelve we are able to see more clearly than before a distinct culmination of some types of play and the origin of other types.   For example, the imitation of single objects as "sandbug," "grasshopper," "wild hog," "policeman," and so forth, had already passed its zenith before the beginning of this period, but social imitation, playing school, store, housekeeping, etc., still holds its sway until about the tenth year, when it begins to decline.   According to Monroe, three-fourths of such plays are by children under eleven years of age.   The same is true of the rhythmic games, such as ring-round-rosy, and farmer-in-the-dell, which in the early part of the period appealed so strongly to the children, especially to the girls.[35]

Subjective Phase

After the ninth year, toys used simply as toys give way to those which require some skill in manipulating, such as stilts, skates, marbles—but "marbles are rarely mentioned after thirteen," "croquet reaches the height of popularity at thirteen." About the beginning of this period, riddles and guessing games culminate in interest, puzzles from ten to twelve, and geometric puzzles at the thirteenth year. In these, and in most of the other games, "the child desires not only power to do, but aims at quickness, dexterity, endurance, accuracy. He holds before himself a certain standard of excellence." "Perception, memory, and reproduction are not only used but tested."[10] "Games requiring some thought, such as 'twelve-men-o'-Morris,' begin to come into favor."[3]

Moreover, the delight, not only in muscular activity, but activity of a very vigorous type, becomes very marked. At six only 11 per cent of all games mentioned are games of chase; after the eighth year such games outnumber the others in the ratio of 2:1. Chase games reach their height by ten, and games of contest begin to take their place. The transition from toys to games means not only that organized activities, that is, play which has set rules, supplants, in a measure, the unorganized activities of early childhood, but social feeling also becomes stronger, as opposed to the marked individualism of the earlier period, in which respect they form a strong contrast.

Meanwhile, the end to be attained in the play has become more remote and complex, and a tendency to form social organizations, in order to accomplish this end, develops during the latter part of this period, which implies also development of life outside the home circle.

We have seen [too] how parental [traditional] influence was still a factor in determining the plays of the Swedish children of Worcester. Here again is a most striking instance of a game, "relievo," nourished and developed until it is mentioned by a third of all the Worcester boys, and yet apparently played but little by the boys of Brooklyn, a little more than one hundred miles distant. But the interesting feature of it all is the substitution of games of the same class. In Brooklyn, "pass walk" and "prisoner's base," appear to be the substitutes for "relievo," while general observation in Chicago and vicinity puts "Pomp, pomp pull-away" in its place.[10]

Summary.—Summing up, now, the psychical characteristics of the children's play during the years seven to twelve, the following appear to be the most marked:

1. A great number and variety as compared with the preceding periods.

2. During the first half of the period, great interest in dramatic plays, housekeeping, store, etc., then a decline from that time onward.

3. The social element of play has become very much more important, especially after the tenth or eleventh year.

4. The interest in performing simple feats, such as turning somersaults,

juggling, and so forth, prominent in the beginning of the period, gradually gives way to chase games which reach their height in popularity at ten, then gradually themselves give way to group games of contest, which, however, do not attain their greatest influence until during the next period.

5. A very marked characteristic of the games of competition, especially prominent in the first half of the period, is the ideal which the child holds before himself of dexterity, quickness, endurance, or accuracy, that is to say, a definite, conscious self-training in motor adjustment and control.

6. The simple guessing games which were played at the beginning of the period are soon replaced by those of a more intellectual type, for example, twelve-men-o'-Morris, checkers, authors, and various other games of cards.

7. As in the first and second periods the activities were instinctive in type, so also in the third group we still find the growing body determining the *type* of physical reactions, but superimposed upon these are the molding influences of tradition, and of differentiation due to sex preferences. Gulick says of this period:

In the main this group of activities starts in most individuals between seven and twelve. It is a higher group of interests than those that ripen in the earlier stage. . . . . It is a gradual shading off of emphasis from a group of activities whose center of interest is one's self to a group whose center of interest is one's self in relation to others. . . . . In the main . . . . more complex intellectual activities are involved—competition is a characteristic of nearly all of these plays. More complicated muscular movements are involved, and a higher degree of foresight than in the first group.

Many of the movements of this group become reflex, but they are reflexes of a very high order, so high that we usually do not call them reflexes. These activities we may characterize as due to tradition, for while we find such activities among all children, they vary among the different classes far more than do the activities of the first group. The tradition of the group of boys determines the specific direction that the interest of the individual should take. . . . . We may further characterize this group as constituting in a general sense the play life of the young of all higher races; they vary in different parts of the world but the bodily and mental qualities demanded by these sports are virtually the same in Africa and England, in China and America. The richness of these plays varies . . . . but these are questions of degree, and not of kind. . . . . [Tag] plays are found in various forms all over the world. They are played by all races of people, although it appears that among the lower peoples they are not taken up by so young children as they are among those that are further advanced.[23]

8. The games of this period differ very much between boys and girls— a differentiation that is far more marked than it is in the earlier group.

Hughlings Jackson already quoted speaks of the spinal cord and of the lower part of the brain as the "lower level" of the nervous system. It is the reflex level. The second level of development is the "sensori-motor" brain, and comprises about one-third of the cortex. The chief years for the development of this second level are during what I have characterized as the middle period . . . . the years from seven to twelve. All the finer motor and sensory development find their chief growth during these years. The upper level, so called, by this theory has to do apparently more with the inhibiting and co-ordinating capacity of the brain.[23]

Biological Phase *(marginal note)*

FOURTH PERIOD—TWELVE TO SEVENTEEN

At sixteen the chase games which were so prominent a feature in the preceding period have fallen to less than 4 per cent., while contest games have come in to take their place. At thirteen one-third of all the games are of contest, and the proportion steadily rises until at sixteen they are to other games as 4:1. Meanwhile, the end to be attained in the game has become more remote. After thirteen the interest in puzzles declines. In their questionnaires, the boys and girls of about this age begin to give reasons for this or that interest, indicating that the critical judgment is becoming active. From ten to fourteen predatory and athletic and military societies greatly increase in number. A stronger tendency to withdraw from the home circle is shown. Strife for mastery is more characteristic of boys; the quieter type of contests, furnished in cards, is more characteristic of girls.

Factual Phase *(marginal note)*

Gulick says of this period:

Coming now to our third major division, we find still more highly organized plays and games. These begin approximately at twelve. . . . . They may begin earlier or may be postponed; in some individuals they doubtless never begin. Attention is called to the characteristics of this group of games—baseball, basketball, football, cricket, hockey are the chief games of the Anglo-Saxon young man. The plays of the period are usually done in gangs or groups, which show the aggregating capacity of the Saxon. Boys have their pals, homogeneous groups that maintain their personnel often for years. It is peculiarly the time for hero worship, and for its characterization by the plays of the period. All of these games and plays show the instinct for co-operation. The games all demand that the individual subordinate himself to the group. *Team work is the keynote* of this group as individual excellence was of the preceding. I do not mean by this that boys always do team work, for they do not. I do mean that that is the ideal that these games represent, without which it is impossible to secure superiority. Little boys will play football and seem to violate this orderly development that otherwise obtains . . . . (but) team work is comparatively rare. Football and baseball, as played by little boys, is a game of individual excellence, each player doing as well as he possibly can, but not sacrificing himself for the sake of the team in which he is playing. . . . .

These plays demand a higher degree of mental and moral qualities than do the preceding. The captain of a team must exercise qualities of a high order, analo-

Subjective Phase
gous to those exercised by a successful chief. We note then, two major elements, co-ordination and self-sacrifice. . . . . Savages who have reached the stage of co-operation are doing that which the Anglo-Saxon boy commences to do soon after he is twelve. . . . . These group activities involve not merely the subordination of self and elevation of the group, but the pursuit of a distant end by means of definite steps, usually indirect, having a more or less definite program; involve obedience to a leader, even when he is evidently mistaken; involve self-control, loyalty to the group as a whole, and in varying degrees, the despising of pain and of individual discomfort. . . . . Those activities that call for the highest things in boy life, that arouse the most passionate enthusiasm, are those that involve this group activity—loyalty to college or country, some objective end rather than a subjective one. . . . .

Recent investigations of Flechsig and other observers have shown that the period commencing about twelve corresponds in the development of the brain to

Biological Phase
the particular growth of the so-called tangential fibers, connecting the different parts of the cortex. These tangential fibers are exceedingly fine, occur in three main layers and are related prominently to those parts of the brain that are neither sensory nor motor. They are association fibers. Flechsig now goes on into the realm of what is not demonstrated, and maintains that those areas of the brain are for association purposes, and hence he characterizes them as association areas. And further, that all the higher capacity in the individual in higher directions is related to this associational area development. This certainly fits in with observed facts, that independent eason has its chief pulse of growing life, beginning with approximately the same year—twelve—as do these tangential fibers. 23

[Kaiser found that the number of developed neurons in the cervical enlargement in man more than doubled from birth to the fifteenth year and twice as many in the right hand as in the left.]

FIFTH PERIOD—YEARS SEVENTEEN TO TWENTY-THREE

During later adolescence—seventeen to twenty-three—there is a development of these same plays and games, but they are sufficiently different, so as, I think,

Factual Phase
to warrant making a separate group of them. The plays are pushed to the limit of endurance and strength, as they are not during the earlier adolescent period. . . . . There is a depth and intensity about it that older people can hardly realize, unless they have been through it.

[Perhaps the most marked psychological characteristic of this period is growing willingness to endure all extremes of hardship in accomplishing self-imposed

Subjective Phase and dangerous tasks in order that the "team" or "college" or "society" may win. There is a growing feeling that "group" interests are something more worthy of sacrifice than mere personal

victory. May it not be that, as the author just quoted suggests, this shifting of
motive, from purely egoistic interests to the interests of a group, is the forerunner
of the truly altruistic spirit soon to manifest itself in obedience to the obligations
of home, society, and country?]

The whole nervous and muscular apparatus, having been fairly well con-
structed during later childhood and adolescence, is now tested and knitted together
with vigor and given endurance and staying power.

Biological Phase [Seventeen is the year when boys are growing most rapidly. The lungs reach their maximum weight about twenty.]

[*Summary.*]—Comparing now the three major groups—early childhood, later
childhood, and adolescence—it appears that the plays of early childhood are
individualistic, non-competitive, and for the accomplishment and observation of
objective results. The plays of later childhood are individualistic, competitive,
involve active muscular co-ordinations and sense judgments. The plays of later
adolescence are socialistic, demanding the heathen virtues of courage, endurance,
self-control, bravery, loyalty, enthusiasm, and the savage occupations of hunting,
fishing, swimming, rowing, sailing. . . . .

*Plays are progressive and that which is the greatest fun at one time is not at
another, because the life itself is progressive.* . . . . .[23]*

Suggestive Summary

1. Babyhood
(AGE APPROXIMATELY 1–3)

Spontaneous involuntary movements of head,
hands, legs, body.
Voluntary movements.
General activities basal, i.e., those which will
be used so constantly throughout life as
to become reflex.
Reflex imitation marked.
Volition appears in choosing between un-
pleasant and pleasant experiences.
Growing control of muscles.
Delight in sensory stimulation.
Type of play instinctive.
A world of sensation and involuntary re-
sponse.
*Spinal cord and "lower level" of brain come
into almost complete activity.*

*Italics mine.

2 EARLY CHILDHOOD
(AGE APPROXIMATELY 3–7)

Activities similar to above, but more complex.
Muscles stronger.
Play largely instinctive. Almost constant activity.
Growing delight in rhythmic stimulation.
Imitation, both reflex and voluntary, very strongly developed.
Great absorption in play.
Little differentiation between play and reality.
The world a world of sensation, perception, apperception.
Individualistic rather than co-operative.
Brain reaches nearly full size.

3. LATER CHILDHOOD
(AGE APPROXIMATELY 7–12)

Running games and others requiring vigorous exercise strongly characteristic.
Dramatization, i.e., social imitation very strong.
Games of skill, i.e., self-training, and games of competition, very characteristic.
The end in play more remote than in previous group.
The period of greatest number and variety of games.
Great interest in "stunts."
Amusements "traditional," and *games* rather than play.
Beginning of social organizations.
Some co-operation.
Intellectual plays, e.g., riddles, puzzles, board games.
Sensation, perception, apperception, and the "practical" judgment, all active.
Slight differentiation of play between the sexes.
Chief period of development of sensori-motor brain.

4. EARLY ADOLESCENCE
(AGE APPROXIMATELY 12-17)

Somatic activity great.
Chase games give way to games of contest.
Sex difference in choice of games is marked.
Life outside the home circle becomes more attractive.
"Group games," "gangs," "societies" and "teams," replace "individual" play. Organizations permanent as well as temporary.
Perception, apperception, critical judgment, active.
Chief development of "association fibers" of brain.

5. LATER ADOLESCENCE
(AGE APPROXIMATELY 17-23)

Plays similar but more intense—pushed to limit of endurance.
Socialistic elements predominant.
Social judgment and reasoning powers active.
The world a world of ideals.
Companions tested by ordeals.
Seventeen the year of most rapid growth for boys.
Lungs reach maximum weight about twenty.
Somatic growth almost completed by end of period.

VI

COMPARISON OF SAVAGE PLAY WITH SUCCESSIVE PERIODS OF CHILDREN'S PLAY

With such fidelity as available data have made possible (1) we have now determined the elements of the play characteristics of five representative savage tribes; (2) by the same method we have analyzed the play of five groups of American children from five representative cities and localities of the United States; (3) we have made a general comparison of the two groups of play characteristics; (4) have made a further study of children's play by periods. It will be our next effort (5) to compare the play of our fivefold savage group with each of the periods of child play, in order to find whether it does or does not correspond to *any particular one* of them. So far as can be judged by the analysis of savage play, the Veddahs stand lowest on the list in respect to development, and the Eskimos highest. Many other lines of comparison confirm this view. Whatever category includes these two extremes, then, must of necessity include the other tribes. Let us consider the subject in the light which the study suggested by the three general rubrics of our charts has shed upon the problem. We found that:

1. In all the five groups of savages play is characterized by activity of the whole body. This is also true of every one of the five periods into which the study of civilized children has been divided. Thus far the two fivefold groups correspond.

Somatic Characteristics

2. Both moderate and violent exercise is typical of savage play, as is the case with children, and when we read that the Veddah or Australian dances until he falls exhausted to the ground; that the Yahgans sometimes become so excited in their wrestling matches, and the manoeuvers so brutal, that fatal consequences result (p. 23); and that the Eskimo hugs his opponent with a grip which may cause the blood to gush forth from his mouth, we cannot but think that the "intensity" of the play is very comparable to that of modern "team" games. In this respect it may be said, then, that parallelism between the non-civilized adults and civilized children and youth is complete up to the end of the periods represented on the charts, namely the twenty-third year.

3. With respect to games requiring a delicate sensori-motor co-ordination, and involving special volitional training of the finer muscles, almost

none are found among the Veddahs and Australians, but the arrow contest of the Bushmen indicates exquisite control of arm and hand muscles, and many games of the Eskimos are calculated to train those muscles.

With the children's group, however, there are in addition to such plays, finger plays, vocal plays, visual, tactual, auditory, and perceptual plays, having almost nothing to correspond to them among the non-civilized adults, but which are indulged in by quite young children among civilized peoples. The children also have a larger proportion of running games. These facts *suggest*, at least, a keener sensitivity and somewhat more specialized muscular control on the part of civilized children. Some of the studies which have been made in experimental psychology seem to confirm this view[45a] but the subject will be further discussed in a future paper already referred to.

The most characteristic types of play organization in our non-civilized group are described by the words "Individual" and "Homogeneous" groups, and "Unorganized Play," but the "Double Homo-

Organization geneous Group" also finds representation in at least three of the tribes, Australians, Bushmen, and Eskimos, and the Eskimos have a few games in which there is some differentiation of parts. They are so few, however, and so local and so seldom mentioned by the authors who report them, that they cannot be called typical, and some of these, even, are apparently introduced games. In so far then as the organization of play is comparable to any particular periods of the children's series, it would seem to correspond most nearly to the third and to the earlier part of the fourth, that is, to the years between seven and fifteen.

The parallelism is not complete, however, for long before the end of this period civilized children are showing a considerable tendency to organize themselves into societies, both spontaneous and formal. Moreover, boys and girls who have reached the age of fifteen have long since dropped such childish plays as "making faces," cat's-cradle, etc., unless for the sake of amusing younger children, while they are still retained by the savages as amusements for adults.

In the psychological characteristics of play, however, we find the greatest disparity between the two groups.

Psychological Characteristics

1. The difference in complexity is very great.

2. "Sensory elements," "rhythm," "mimicry," "dramatic representation," "skill," "the practical judgment," "individual competition," are the characteristics which stand out with great emphasis in the study of the phylogenetic group, and these qualities are strongly characteristic of the civilized children, in the years from approximately seven to thirteen or fourteen.

3. But American children have along with these plays many others in which purely intellectual activity is the attractive element—guessing games, charades, puzzles, geographical games, etc.—a class finding no representation whatever among the tribes here studied. The intellectual elements of the savage play correspond much more nearly to those of American children from six to ten years of age; yet civilized children younger than that enjoy simple intellectual plays. That this difference in types extends farther than mere play, that it is a real and not apparent attitude of mind, may be shown, perhaps, by one or two brief character sketches, introduced as supplementary evidence. The first is from the pen of Commodore Peary, whose long familiarity with the Eskimos makes his opinion particularly valuable. He says:

Through all this laborious work, my happy, child-like crew was a constant source of interest to me. During the first two days of the voyage, they had been very quiet . . . . but now, well within the limits of "Ikaresungwah" (Whale Sound), and hugging the shore within a boat's length, they were garrulous as so many sparrows. The regular stroke of the oars seemed an incentive to continuous chatter. Spicy gossip of the tribe, the wonderful ship, incidents of our voyage, speculations as to my plans, apostrophes to the waves, the sky, the birds—an incessant stream. Never did an inquisitive burgomaster gull stoop with wide white wings to inspect the boat but what he was chaffed and derided; not a flock of bustling little auks whirred past but they were followed by encouraging words equivalent to "Go it, little ones," "That's right," "You'll get there"; and the sight of a seal's glistening black head emerging from the water would be the signal for a volley of *Taku! Taku! Taku-u-u!* ("Look") *Puisse!* in inimitable accents, and as much excitement as if it was the first seal of their lives. Yet at a word of caution from me the noise would cease, the broad backs strain and sway till the oars bent like whalebone, and the boat forged slowly through the boiling tide-rip round a projecting point.[43]

The second quotation is from Rasmussen, who, having spent his boyhood among the Eskimos, and who being familiar with their language, understands them, perhaps, as well as any white man living.

When the young Eskimo grows into a man—and that happens the day it dawns upon him that his childish play can be taken in earnest; that he might just as well close upon a real bear as with the carved blocks of ice he used to play with; that he might just as well steal up to a real seal as to a make-believe one— he is filled with only one desire: to be equal to the others, the best of them; and this becomes his life ambition. All his thoughts are thus centered on hunting expeditions, seal-catching, fishing, food. Beyond this, thought is as a rule associated with care.

Once out hunting, I asked an Eskimo, who seemed to be plunged in reflection, "What are you standing there thinking about?" He laughed at my question, and said: "Oh! it is only you white men who go in so much for thinking; up here we only think of our flesh-pits and of whether we have enough or not for the long dark of the winter. If we have meat enough then there is no need to think. I have meat and to spare!" I saw that I had insulted him by crediting him with thought.

On another occasion I asked an unusually intelligent Eskimo, Panigpak, who had taken part in Peary's last North Polar Expedition [1898–1902],

"Tell me, what do you suppose was the object of all your exertions? What did you think when you saw the land disappear behind you, and you found yourself out on drifting ice-floes?"

"Think?" said Panigpak, astonished, "I did not need to think. Peary did that!"

During the year I spent with the Polar Eskimos, there was comfort and plenty everywhere, and, so far as I could ascertain, this was the usual state of affairs. Thus what they ask of life they receive, and their requirements being satisfied, an irresponsible happiness at merely being alive finds expression in their actions and conversation. They have all sorts of sudden impulses, and are free to follow them up unchecked. They are now here, now there, incalculable in their whims, now on dangerous and arduous hunting or sealing expeditions, now at jovial entertainments, and are touchingly grateful for a jest or joke.[44]

VII

CONCLUSIONS

1. In view of the facts herein presented, *regarding play activities, we conclude, then, that although a similarity certainly exists between the play* With Respect *of the child race and of the child individual, especially with* to *respect to somatic characteristics, yet a process of differentiation* Parallelism *has been going on throughout the cultural period which has profoundly modified not only the final product, i.e., the product found in civili zation, but also all the intervening stages. It is our belief that this differentiation is shown, to a slight extent, in the physical organism itself, so that the physical body of the highest type found in civilization is somewhat more sensitive to stimulation than is the body of the highest type of savage. This opinion is not based, however, entirely upon the study of play, but partly upon a supplementary study on "Somatic Characteristics."*

The chief difference appears, however, in the intellectual aspects of their amusements, and is a difference not of kind but of proportions, or we may say a difference of emphasis. Thus we find in the play of our non-civilized group somatic activities and emotional intensity characterizing civilized children and youth between the ages of six and twenty-three, a form of organization more nearly corresponding to the period from six to twelve or thirteen, and purely intellectual play somewhat comparable to that of civilized children from six to eleven years old, i.e., the time when spontaneous imitation, and dramatization of social activities, maintains its highest interest, and when skill for its own sake and rivalry are the compelling motives in play. The studies on the ordeal, courtship, and religious plays are confirmatory of this view. The attitude of mind therein disclosed is the attitude of the child mind, not that of the civilized adult.

2. But the difference of proportions above referred to is not acquired in any given individual by living the life of a savage until the limit of *his* development is reached, *then adding to that product something more,* which extends development in ontogenesis to the point reached in civilization. *The differentiation in parallelism is much more fundamental, reaching back to the beginnings of psychical life, and probably far back into the physical organism itself.*

The theory of psychical evolution thus presented, namely that while in any given period of ontogenetic development the psychology of children's play resembles, in certain respects, the psychology of savage play, *yet at no point is like it*, seems to us so entirely in accord with a recent statement of theory regarding somatic embryonic evolution,[32] that we cannot forbear to quote the statement at length.   Professor Lillie says:

Haeckel's formula, that the development of the individual repeats briefly the evolution of the species, or that ontogeny is a brief recapitulation of phylogeny, has been widely accepted by embryologists.   It is based on a comparison between the embryonic development of the individual and the comparative anatomy of the phylum.   The embryonic conditions of any set of organs of a higher species of a phylum resemble, in many essential particulars, conditions that are adult in lower species of the same phylum; and, moreover, the order of embryonic development of organs corresponds in general to the taxonomic order of organization of the same organs.   As the taxonomic order is the order of evolution, Haeckel's generalization, which he called the fundamental law of biogenesis, would appear to follow of necessity.

But it never happens that the embryo of any definite species resembles in its entirety the adult of a lower species, nor even the embryo of a lower species; its organization is specific at all stages from the ovum on, so that it is possible without any difficulty to recognize the order of animals to which a given embryo belongs, and more careful examination will usually enable one to assign its zoölogical position very closely.

If phylogeny be understood to be the succession of adult forms in the line of evolution, it cannot be said in any real sense that ontogeny is a brief recapitulation of phylogeny, for the embryo of a higher form is never like the adult of a lower form, though the anatomy of embryonic organs of higher species resembles in many particulars the anatomy of homologous organs of the adult of the lower species. However, if we conceive that the whole life history is necessary for the definition of a species, we obtain a different basis for the recapitulation theory.   The comparable units are then entire ontogenies, and these resemble one another in proportion to the nearness of relationship, just as the definitive structures do. The ontogeny is inherited no less than the adult characteristics, and is subject to precisely the same laws of modification and variation.   Thus in nearly related species the ontogenies are very similar; in more distantly related species there is less resemblance, and in species from different classes the ontogenies are widely divergent in many respects.

In species of lower grades of organization the ontogenetic series is a shorter one than in species of higher grades, so that the final stages of the organs of a lower species become intermediate or embryonic stages in species of higher rank. But the stage of the lower species does not appear in all the organs of the higher species simultaneously.   Thus the fish never exhibits the grade of organization of a fish throughout; while its pharynx, for instance, is in a fish-like condition with reference to arches and clefts, the nervous system is relatively undifferentiated, and it has no vertebrae; on the other hand, it has a heart of an amphibian rather than of a fish type.

Some of these considerations may be represented graphically as follows: let us take a species D that has an ontogeny A, B, C, D, and suppose that this species evolves successively into species E, F, G, H, etc. When evolution has progressed a step, to E, the characters of the species established develop directly from the ovum, and are therefore, in some way, involved in the composition of the latter. All of the stages of the ontogeny leading up to E are modified, and we can indicate this in the ontogeny of E as in line 2:

1. $A\ B\ C\ D$
2. $A^1\ B^1\ C^1\ D^1\ E$
3. $A^2\ B^2\ C^2\ D^2\ E^1\ F$
4. $A^3\ B^3\ C^3\ D^3\ E^2\ F^1\ G$
5. $A^4\ B^4\ C^4\ D^4\ E^3\ F^2\ G^1\ H$

Similarly, when evolution has progressed to species F, seeing that the characters of F now develop directly from the ovum, all the ontogenetic stages leading up to F are modified, line 3. And so on for each successive advance in evolution, lines 4 and 5. It will also be noticed that the terminal stage D of species 1 becomes a successively earlier ontogenetic stage of species 2, 3, 4, 5, etc., and moreover, it does not recur in its pure form, but in the form D^1 in species 2, D^2 in species 3, etc. Now if the last five stages of the ontogeny of species 5 be examined, viz., $D^4\ E^3\ F^2\ G^1\ H$, it will be seen that they repeat the phylogeny of the adult stages D E F G H, but in a modified form.

This is in fact what the diagram shows; but it is an essential defect of the diagram, that it is incapable of showing the character of the modifications of the ancestral conditions. Not only is each stage of the ancestral ontogenies modified with each phylogenetic advance, but the elements of organization of the ancestral stages are also dispersed so that no ancestral stage hangs together as a unit. The embryonic stages show as much proportional modification in the course of evolution as the adult, but this is not so obvious owing to the simpler and more generalized character of the embryonic stages.

In the acceptation of the foreoing conclusions regarding the comparative play characteristics of savage adults and civilized children it must be kept in mind, that:

1. We are not discussing the development of the above-named groups as a whole, but only that phase which represents the spontaneous, recreative side of life. The suggestion is indeed strong, that the characteristics here found extend much farther than to mere play activities, but final conclusions relating to psychical phenomena other than play impulses must await the completion of supplementary studies.

2. We are not discussing what the members of our fivefold groups are *capable* of playing, but what they *play*. Whether the same tribes reared under exactly the same conditions as civilized children would have developed exactly the same capacities and inclinations as the latter class is an entirely

different question, and one not even touched in this discussion. The question suggests an inviting field of experimental research, but surely it is of some value to know these people *as they are*, not only for those who propose to make their life work among peoples little civilized, either as teachers or as missionaries, but for a nation which has already put itself on record as a champion of weaker races. What a splendid tool for education might all of these find in the much-loved drama of the savage!

3. The conclusions here expressed as to tastes and inclinations in play must not be construed as applying to *all* savage tribes. The study is purposely confined to some of the lowest in development.

Reviewing, now, the various lines of thought by which the end of our discussion has been reached, we are confronted at length by the questions, What is play? What is its genesis?

With Respect to Genesis of Play It is not our purpose here to present again the various theories already before the public. Spencer's theory that play is due to an *excess of energy* in unused brain centers, which discharges itself in play activities, is true to the extent that energy is certainly present and expended during such activity; but why "excess" of energy?

The theory of Groos that play activities are *anticipatory* (i.e., a drill or training for adult life) has certainly so much of truth as this—play does so train. But why does the child in his ignorance of adult needs react in just those ways which do thus train him? The explanation needs itself to be explained.

And lastly we have the theory of Dr. G. Stanley Hall that the child recapitulates psychical interests and activities of the race, as well as physical structure, through *inheritance*. *Something* certainly is inherited, or there would be no child to play; but if the child's psychical interests develop in the order in which the race developed them, why does he take pleasure in the whistle of his toy engine long before he begs for bow and arrow or fishing rod?

Without denying a portion of truth to all these theories, we venture to suggest a fourth, which possibly may be allowed a place beside the other three—a theory which may perhaps be called

THE BIOLOGICAL THEORY OF PLAY

Does not the growing body itself provide its own best explanation of the fact of play? (1) *Sensitivity to stimulation*, and (2) *power of reaction to stimulation* seem to characterize all forms of living matter. But *the structure of the body places limitations* upon the *kind* of reaction which it is possible to make. A kitten cannot react to a pool of water as the fish does, nor can the fish take on the reactions of the kitten. From the standpoint of both fish and kitten, such a procedure would be as undesirable as it is impossible. Both animals react as did their ancestors, because limitations of bone, muscle, tendons, nerves, and vital organs necessitate their acting, if they act at all, in just those ways and in no others. Just so the child being built upon the same general plan as were his ancestors must of necessity use the same muscles and organs and in about the same way, and in so doing both recapitulates his phylogenetic inheritance and anticipates his ontogenetic future in those plays which have been called "instinctive," and which are especially typical of infancy and early childhood. All that is needed then to account for *"instinctive"* play is the impulse to *act*, and this he has at birth, endowed as he is with sensitivity to stimulation. For the rest, the child's environment, both physical and social, pours in upon his sensorium a constant stream of stimulation, *suggesting the particular act of the immediate present.* But the *type* of the activity *is determined by the stage of development which the growing body has reached.* With the infant, the head and arm muscles, being strongest, control the somatic type of play, together with the developing sense-organs of the nervous system and the brain. *Sensations*, coming through the sheen of light, the shake of the rattle, the throwing of the ball, are his mental toys and his delight. Later, when stronger muscles co-operate in stronger and more complex movements and when further brain development makes perception and apperception possible, activity of the whole body is the somatic type, while mentally *imagination, volition,* and *imitation* become his toys. And so we hear, "Tell me a story," and see, a little later, the story epitomized in dramatic representation.

Meanwhile, the brain having reached nearly its full size, a period of slower brain growth follows, and bones, muscles, and lungs take their turn at rapid growth. Just now comes in the period of "running games," "tag," "hunting games," etc., with rivalry and skill as toys, only to be followed by "contest" games and co-operative groups, necessitating adjustment of means to ends, at just that period of life when tangential fibers uniting the various centers of the brain are developing most rapidly, and all the organs of the body are maturing.

Why does the desire for this violent exercise pass away as the body ceases growing, and why do intellectual and business occupations gradually become, not merely necessary, but really more congenial? May we not safely assume that in the normal, well-ordered life the brain continues to develop in histological structure long after somatic growth has ceased, and that with the increasing complexity of brain structure, not acts, but the *relations* of acts, the abstract reasoning, the constructive imagination become the *toy* of the adult, as sensation, perception, skill, conquest, and co-operation for distant ends have been in the past? Is it not significant that whatever the type of play may be, *it just keeps pace with the type of somatic growth?* And does not the impulse to exercise these growing parts furnish all the explanation that is needed for the existence of the play activity?

But *why the impulse* to exercise the growing organs?

The tissues grow by means of chemical elements brought to them by the blood. The more rapid the heart beat the more rapid the circulation of blood and therefore the greater the food supply brought to the tissues. It is an interesting fact that even the normal heart beat is quicker in the growing child than in the adult. Possibly it is *because* of the greater demand of the tissues in the *growing* child that this is so; and tissue-demand-for-more-food (*tissue hunger*, if we will) may be only another name for play impulse. The child does not understand *why* he likes to run better than to sit still any more than he understands why he likes to stretch himself after he has slept so soundly that the heart has slowed its beat and the brain has ceased functioning. But the stretch of the muscles quickens the heart beat once more, the yawn brings oxygen to the lungs, and soon the drowsy brain, supplied with better food, is functioning again.

Just so in playing tag, the child is quickening the circulation of the blood and feeding bone and lungs and tissues with chemical elements necessary for their growth. He feels only the impulse to *do*, to move, to fidget. If opportunity for play be denied, the *impulse* remains still, and frequently expends itself in mischief or "incorrigibility," but if *all* exercise be denied, then the growing tissues must suffer the unavoidable consequences of partial starvation. Back of psychological impulses are physiological functions; back of physiological functions are histological changes; and back of histological changes are chemical attractions and repulsions.

With respect to "*traditional*" games, we have already anticipated the theory, namely that they have their genesis in experience—*somebody's* experience—and that they are handed down from generation to generation. As the dramatic element of the original play drops out and is forgotten, it gradually becomes conventionalized into a game of skill. The more varied the history of the people the more experiences, and hence the more traditions to be handed down.

But this conclusion with respect to play, both instinctive and traditional, brings us face to face with a larger question still., *Play is an instinct.* Is instinct, then, due only to chemical attraction, tissue hunger, structure, stimulation, imitation, and tradition?

If this be true, then instinct is but another name for hunger. If this be true, then instinct is post-natal as well as pre-natal. It is constructive, not passive. It is determinative, not determined. It is dynamic, not static. It is volitional as well as reflex, and the controversy as to whether instinct is "relapsed volitional action," or whether it is purely "reflex" is forever brushed aside. It is both; it is neither.

The pedagogical inferences from our study of play are so apparent as hardly to need the emphasis of repetition.

With Respect to Pedagogical Applications

1. Any system of education which leaves out of account the "hungers" of the child, both physical and psychical, leaves also out of account his whole development.

2. The play hunger is but one of many. The greater the variety of normal hungers, the more developed the child. But the *type of hungers, not the number of his years,* indicates the extent of his development. True, mind and body alike may be starved or over-stimulated, until they are unbalanced or until they cease to function normally, but these are pathological cases and do not fall within the scope of this discussion.

3. Some of these normal hungers are indicated in the analysis of children's play—hunger for exercise, for social appreciation, imitation, organization, sensation, rhythm, self-training, competition, co-operation, fun, intellectual activity, companionship, and religion—all these, and others which may be determined, are the impelling forces by which development will be accomplished and personality and character shaped.

4. These cravings are more than mere incidental likes and dislikes. They indicate the degree of health and growth which mind and body have attained.

5. A hunger unsatisfied, over-stimulated, perverted, or fed upon injurious food can only result in arrest of development.

6. The duty of pedagogy is to place before the hungry pupil food suited to the normal appetite. Not one of the ingredients named above can be omitted from the menu. For the abnormal appetite specialists are needed who can give each case as careful consideration as does the skilled physician to his patients.

7. The proportions in which the ingredients of mental diet should be mixed must change with changing development. The proportions which normal children use themselves when strongly interested will be the teacher's best guide.

8. The study of less-developed types of humanity, both civilized and

non-civilized, will be an invaluable aid to the teacher, not only in quickening his own sympathy and capability of helpful service to society in general, but in placing at his command a vast fund of knowledge and of facts which may be made directly useful for instruction. To understand the part which instinct has played in the promotion of civilization, the process by which impulsive, objective acts have become subjective, abstract, social, altruistic, is to know how to direct the child's longings so as to create a further hunger for worthy, progressive, heroic living, rather than for satisfaction in mean and sordid aims.

9. That children's stories, poems, and songs, the type of pictures they make, their emotions, their attitude toward punishment, authority, and law, their critical judgment, their belief in charms, their ideals, and even their plays are subject to laws which apply alike to the Bushman, the Chinese, and the American is just as surely established as is the fact that the periods of slow and rapid physical growth and the changing proportions of the body are subject to law. The pedagogy of the future must be based upon these laws.

Some of a child's deeds are symptoms of a waning tendency; they are survivals in functioning of an organ which has done its part and is passing out of vital use. To give positive attention to such qualities is to arrest development upon a lower level. It is systematically to maintain a rudimentary phase of growth. Other activities are signs of a culminating power and interest; to them applies the maxim of striking while the iron is hot. As regards them it is, perhaps, a matter of now or never. Selected, utilized, emphasized, they may mark a turning-point for good in the child's whole career. Neglected, an opportunity goes never to be recalled. Other acts and feelings are prophetic; they represent the dawning of a flickering light that will shine steadily only in the far future. As regards them there is little at present to do but give them fair and full chance, waiting for the future for definite direction.[15]

10. The Culture Epoch Theory is, perhaps, the first really scientific effort to take advantage of race experience for the benefit of the child; but its followers have sometimes erred in that they have confused the type of the reaction with the conditions which stimulate reaction, and have thought to secure the benefits of race experience by introducing the child into the specific activities of the primitive peoples or into a similar environment. To take this view is certainly to seize upon the husk and throw away the kernel. It is not the thing done, but the *way* it is done that is significant. The *psychology* of the reaction is the all-important thing, and we shall find that the psychology of the reaction takes on a different type as we rise in the developmental series. In whatever direction the mind expresses itself, the

act will take on that type belonging to its specific period of development. Thus if it be the period when the sensori-motor type predominates, not only will the play be of that type, but literature, art, religion. As a matter of fact, many of the games and dances are religious in character, but it is religion expressed in terms of muscle, rather than in passive forms of abstract philosophy. And this is as it should be. Religious and moral ideas, dissociated from muscular expression, become hypocrisy. Many a mission field bears witness to the failure of attempting to force a subjective type of religion upon a sensori-motor type of mind; yet in educational matters the mission schools have been wise beyond their age in laying much stress upon the industrial, that is, the motor phase.

11. Thus with both child and race, the all-important thing for both parent and instructor is to learn to know the type. If we study carefully the actual activities of these lowest tribes and the activities of civilized children we find very little in common between them except these types, these changing mental attitudes which manifest themselves in all the relations of life. It is not a hunting instinct, as some have supposed, which the child inherits, but a hunger instinct—hunger for food and hunger for sensation. Whatever satisfies that appetite will call forth the typical reaction just as quickly, whether the stimulus belongs to modern life or to primitive conditions. So it is not the migratory instinct but the motor instinct which impels the child to wander into the woods or snowball his playmates with equal zest. It is not because a myth is a myth that the children listen to the narrator with such rapt attention, but because it is objective, striking, full of visual imagery, dramatic, the characters few, the relations simple, the forms of thought concrete, dealing little with subjective, abstract themes. But any other story which has these same characteristics, that is, *the same type*, will hold attention equally well.

12. The value of the study of the culture epochs, then, is primarily for the teacher, not for the child, because in them are found supplementary studies of mental types, each one of which will throw some light upon the diagnosis of the special case in hand. To understand the race is to better understand the child.

13. Do the culture epochs, then, yield no direct products for the pupil, as well as for the teacher?

The world is the child's; its people his people; its interests his interests. No mind is "cultured" which does not acknowledge its debt to the mind of the primitive folk. No education is "broad" which does not recognize the skill and patience and beauty of the primitive industries and products. To bring a knowledge of these and a sympathetic interest therewith into the child's life, it is necessary to bring the specific products of the culture epochs corresponding most nearly to his own, into the realm of formal instruction. But to do this intelligently, it is necessary that the teacher add to his knowledge of genetic pedagogy a genetic anthropology; to his genetic psychology a genetic somatology, and for a curriculum based upon textbooks and years of school attendance, must be substituted one based upon TYPES OF DEVELOPMENT, including both Mind and Body.

VIII

BIBLIOGRAPHY

The following authorities have been consulted in preparing this monograph. Many minor articles have been omitted, the aim of the author being to include only such as possessed intrinsic value. We regret that Seligmann's exhaustive study of the Veddahs has not yet appeared in print.

Astrup, Edwind. "In the Land of the Northernmost Eskimos," *Fortnightly Review*, LXV, N.S. London. [1]

Avebury, Lord (Sir John Lubbock). *Prehistoric Times, as Illustrated by Ancient Remains and the Manners and Customs of Modern Savages*. 5th ed. London, Edinburgh: Williams & Norgate, 1890. 616 pages; illustrated.

Babcock, W. H. "Games of Washington Children," *American Anthropologist*, I (1888), 243–84. Washington, D.C.: Judd & Detweiler, 1888. [2]

Bailey, John. "An Account of the Wild Tribes of the Veddahs of Ceylon, Their Habits, Customs, and Superstitions," *Transactions of the Ethnological Society of London*, II, N.S. 1863. [3]

Baldwin, James Mark. *Mental Development in the Child and the Race—Methods and Processes*. New York and London: Macmillan, 1895. 406 pages. [4]

Barker, Lewellys Franklin. *The Nervous System and Its Constituent Neurons: Designed for the Use of Practitioners of Medicine and Psychology*. New York: D. Appleton & Co., 1899. 1122 pages; illustrated.

Barnes, Earl. *Studies in Education*. 1896–1902, I and II. California, Leland Stanford Junior University, and Philadelphia. [5]

Batson, M. A., F.R.S. *Methods and Scope of Genetics*. Inaugural Lecture Delivered October, 1908. Cambridge: University Press, 1908. 49 pages. [5a]

Bleek, Wilhelm Henrich Immanual. *Brief Account of Bushman Folklore and Other Texts*. London: Trübner, 1875. 21 pages.

Boas, Franz. *Anthropology*. A Lecture Delivered at Columbia University in the Series on Science, Philosophy, and Art, December 18, 1907. New York: Columbia University Press, 1908. 28 pages.

———. "The Anthropology of the North American Indian," *Memoirs of the International Congress of Anthropology*. Edited by C. Staniland Wake. Chicago: Schulte Publishing Co., 1894.

———. "Dissemination of Tales among the Natives of North America," *Journal of American Folk Lore*, IV, 13–20. Boston and New York: Houghton Mifflin Co., 1891.

———. "The Central Eskimo," *Sixth Annual Report of Bureau of American Ethnology* (1884–85), 399–666. [6]

———. "The Half-Blood Indian," *Popular Science Monthly* (1894). New York.

———. "The Indians of British Columbia," *Transactions of Royal Society of Canada*, 51.

———. "Limitations of the Comparative Method of Anthropology," *Science*, IV, N.S., 901.

———. "The Mind of Primitive Man," *Smithsonian Institution, Annual Report* (1901), 451–60, Washington, 1902. Reprinted from *Journal of American Folk Lore*, V, 14 (January–March, 1901).

Bolton, Thaddeus L. "Rhythm," *Pedagogical Seminary*, VI (January, 1899), 153.

Brinton, Daniel Garrison. *Races and Peoples*. Lectures on the Science of Ethnography. New York: Hodges. 313 pages. First published in 1890.

Brown, Robert. "Eskimos," art. in *Encyclopaedia Britannica*, VIII, 543–49. New York: Scribner, 1878. 9th ed.

Bucher, Karl. *Industrial Evolution*. New York: Henry Holt & Co., 1901. 393 pages. [7]

Census of Ceylon (1901), I, 73.

Champlin, John D., and Bostwick, Arthur E. *The Young Folks' Cyclopedia of Games and Sports*. Illustrated. New York: Henry Holt & Co., 1899 2d ed., revised. 784 pages. [7a]

Chase, John H. "Street Games of New York City," *Pedagogical Seminary*, XII (December, 1905), 503–4. [8]

Clodd, E. "Dr. Nansen's First Crossing of Greenland," *Knowledge*, 1891.

Comer, Capt. George. "Whaling in Hudson Bay," *Boas Anniversary Volume*, 483. New York: Stechert & Co., 1906. 559 pages.

Cook, James. *A Voyage toward the South Pole*, II. London: W. Strahan, 1777.

———. *Narrative of the Voyages around the World Performed by Captain James Cook*. New York: Harper. 445 pages.

Cordover, don A de. *Voyage of Discovery to Strait of Magellan*, 99.

Crantz, David. *History of Greenland*. London: Longman & Brown, 1820. [9]

Crosswell, T. R. "Amusements of Worcester School Children," *Pedagogical Seminary* (September, 1899), VI, 314–71. [10]

Culin, Stewart. "Games of the North American Indians," *Twenty-fourth Annual Report of the Bureau of American Ethnology*, Smithsonian Institution, 1902–3. Washington: Government Printing Office, 1907. [11]

———. "Street Games of Boys in Brooklyn, N.Y.," *Journal of American Folk Lore*, IV (1891), 221–37. Boston and New York: Houghton Mifflin Co. [12]

Cunningham, D. J. "The Australian Forehead," *Anthropological Essays*, 65. Edited by N. W. Thomas, in Honor of Edward Burnett Tylor's Seventy-fifth Birthday. Oxford: Clarendon Press, 1907. 416 pages.

Dall, William Healey. "Alaska and Its Resources, 595–609. Boston: Lee & Shepard, 1870. [13]

———. "Tribes of Extreme Northwest," *Contributions to North American Ethnology*, I, 1–156. Washington, 1877.

————. "On Masks, Labrets, and Certain Aboriginal Customs, with an Inquiry into the Bearing of Their Geographical Distribution," *Third Annual Report of the Bureau of American Ethnology*, 67–203. Smithsonian Institution. Washington: Government Printing Office, 1884.

————. "On the Remains of Prehistoric Man, Obtained from Caves in the Catherina Archipelago, Alaska Territory, and Especially from the Caves of the Aleutian Islands," Part I. *Smithsonian Contributions to Knowledge*, XXII, No. 318. Washington, D.C.

————. "Notes on Prehistoric Remains in the Aleutian Islands," *Proceedings of California Academy of Sciences*, November 4, 1872.

————. "Social Life among Our Aborigines," *American Naturalist*, XII. Boston.

Darwin, Charles. *Journal of Researches into the Natural History and Geology of the Countries Visited during the Voyage of H.M.S. "Beagle" round the World under the Command of Captain Fitz-Roy, R.N.*, III. New ed., New York: D. Appleton & Co., 1878. 519 pages. [14]

Deniker, Joseph. *The Races of Man: An Outline of Anthropology and Ethnography.* London: W. Scott; New York: Scribner, 1900. 611 pages.

de Quatrefages, Armand. *The Pigmies.* Trans. by Frederick Starr. London: Macmillan, 1895. 255 pages.

Dewey, John. "Interpretation of the Savage Mind," *Psychological Review*, IX, 217. New York.

————. *The Child and the Curriculum.* Chicago: The University of Chicago Press. [15]

————. *The School and Society.* Three Lectures Given at the University of Chicago. Chicago: The University of Chicago Press, 1907. 129 pages.

————. "Interpretations of the Savage Mind," *Psychological Review*, IX, 217.

DeWindt, Harry. *Through the Gold Fields of Unalaska to Bering Strait.* New York and London: Harper & Bros., 1898. 314 pages.

Donaldson, Henry Herbert. *The Growth of the Brain.* A Study of the Nervous System in Relation to Education. London: W. Scott, 1895. 374 pages; illustrated.

Ellis, Col. A. B. "West African Folk Lore," *Popular Science Monthly.* New York, 1872.

Ellis, A. Caswell, and Hall, G. Stanley. "A Study of Dolls," *Pedagogical Seminary*, IV, No. 2 (December, 1896), 129–75. [16]

Eyre, John Edward. *Discoveries in Central Australia.* [17]

Ferrier, Prof. D. In *Anthropological Institute*, XVII, 33.

Fitz-Roy, Capt. Robert. *Narrative of Surveying Voyages of the "Beagle."* 3 vols. London: H. Colburn, 1839. [18]

Forbes, Henry Ogg. *Eleven Years in Ceylon*, II, 76. 1841.

France, Clemens J. "The Gambling Impulse," *American Journal of Psychology*, XII (July, 1902), 364. Worcester, Mass.: Clark University Press. [19]

Frear, Caroline. "Imitation: A Study Based on E. H. Russel's *Child Observations*," *Pedagogical Seminary*, IV, No. 3 (April, 1897), 382–86. Clark University, Worcester, Mass. [20]

Frobenious, Leo. *The Childhood of Man: A Popular Account of the Lives, Customs and Thoughts of the Primitive Races.* Trans. by A. H. Keane. London: Seeley & Co., Great Russel St., 1909. 504 pages; illustrated.

Garson, J. G. In *Journal of the Anthropological Institute* (1885 and 1886).

Gibbons, Alfred St. Hill. *Africa from North to South.* London and New York: J. Lane, 1904. 2 vols. Maps.

Gomme, Alice Bertha. *Traditional Games of England, Scotland, and Ireland*, II, last chapter. London: David Nutt, 1898.

Gray, George. *Expeditions in Northwest Australia.* [21]

Greely, Adolphus Washington. *Three Years of Arctic Service.* An Account of the Lady Franklin Bay Expedition of 1881–84, and the Attainment of the Farthest North. New York: Scribner, 1886. 2 vols. Illustrations and maps.

Groos, Karl. *The Play of Man.* New York: D. Appleton & Co., 1901.

Grosse, Ernst. *Beginnings of Art.* New York: D. Appleton & Co., 1897. 327 pages; illustrated. [22]

Gulick, Luther, M.D. "Psychological, Pedagogical, and Religious Aspects of Group Games," *Pedagogical Seminary.* [23]

———. "Some Psychical Aspects of Muscular Exercise," *Popular Science Monthly*, LIII (1898), 793–805. New York: D. Appleton & Co. [23]

Gunckel, John E. *Boyville; A History of Fifteen Years' Work among Newsboys.* Toledo, Ohio, Newsboy's Association.

Haddon, Alfred Cort. *The Study of Man.* New York: G. P. Putnam's Sons; London: Bliss, Sands & Co., 1898. 410 pages. [24]

Hall, Granville Stanley. *Adolescence; Its Psychology, and Its Relations to Physiology, Anthropology, Sociology, Sex, Crime, Religion, and Education.* New York: D. Appleton & Co., 1907. 2 vols.

———. "Child-Study the Basis of an Exact Science of Education," *Forum*, XVI (1893–94).

———. *Story of a Sand-Pile.* New York: Kellogg, 1897. 20 pages.

———. *Pedagogical Seminary.* Various numbers. Clark University, Worcester, Mass. [25]

Hartshorn, B. F. In *Fortnightly Review* (1876). London.

Hawkesworth, John. *Account of Voyages in the Southern Hemisphere.* London: Strahan, 1773. 3 vols.

Herbart Year Books.

Hiller, H. M., and Furness, Dr. W. H. *Notes of a Trip to the Veddahs of Ceylon.* London, 1902. 45 pages. [26]

Hobhouse, Leonard Trelawney. *Mind in Evolution.* London and New York: Macmillan, 1901. 415 pages.

———. *Morals in Evolution: A Study in Comparative Ethics.* London: Chapman & Hall, 1906. 2 vols.

Holub, Dr. Emil. *Seven Years in South Africa*, II. London: Sampson Low, & Rivington, 1881. Trans. by Ellen E. Frewer.

Hrdlička, Aleš. "An Eskimo Brain," *American Anthropologist*, III. Washington, 1885.

Hutchinson, Gregory, and Lydekker. *The Living Races of Mankind.* 1903.

Hyades, Paul, and Deniker, J. *Mission scientifique du Cap Horn, 1882–83*, VII. Paris: Gautier, 1891. [27]

James, William. *Principles of Psychology.* New York: Henry Holt & Co., 1902. 2 vols.

Johnson, J. Hemsley. "Rudimentary Societies among Boys," *Johns Hopkins Studies in Historical and Political Science*, 2d S., II, 10. Also issued as a reprint by the "Boys of the McDonogh School" (1893). 66 pages.

Johnston, H. H. *British Central Africa.* London: Methuen & Co., 1898. Maps.

Johnston, Sir Harry Hamilton. "The Pygmies of the Great Congo Forest," *Annual Report of the Smithsonian Institution* (1902), 479–91. Washington, 1903. Reprinted from *McClure's Magazine*, February, 1902.

Kane, Elisha Kent. *Arctic Explorations*, I, II. [28]
——. In *North American Review*. Boston and New York (1857).

Keane, Agustus Henry. *Man, Past and Present.* Cambridge, Eng: The University Press, 1900. Half-title, "Cambridge Geographical Series." 584 pages; illustrated.
——. *Central and South America.* London: E. Stanford, 1901. 2 vols.; illustrations and maps.

Keatly. "Under the Arctic Circle," *Arena*, VII. [29]

Keely, Robert N. *In Arctic Seas with Peary's Expedition.* R. C. Hartranft, 1893. 524 pages; illustrations and maps. [30]

Kidd, Dudley. *The Essential Kaffir.* London: A. C. Black, 1904. 435 pages; illustrations; bibliography.

King, Philip Parker. *Narrative of Surveying Voyage of H.M.S. "Adventure" and "Beagle" between the Years 1826 and 1836.* London: H. Colburn, 1839. 3 vols.; maps.

Kirkpatrick, Edwin Asbury. *Genetic Psychology: An Introduction to an Objective and Genetic View of Intelligence.* New York: Macmillan, 1909, 373 pages. [31]
——. *Fundamentals of Child-Study: A Discussion of Instincts and Other Factors in Human Development, with Practical Applications.* New York: Macmillan, 1903. 384 pages.

Lea, Henry Charles. *Superstition and Force.* Essays on the Wager of Law, the Wager of Battle, the Ordeal, Torture. 4th ed. Philadelphia: Lea, 1892. 627 pages.

Lillie, Frank Rattray. *The Development of the Chick: An Introduction to Embryology.* New York: Henry Holt & Co., 1908. 472 pages. [32]

Lindley, Ernest H. "A Study of Puzzles with Special Reference to the Psychology of Mental Adaptation," *American Journal of Psychology*, VIII, No. 4 (July 1897). Worcester, Mass. [33]

Livingstone, David. *Missionary Travels and Researches in South Africa*. New York: Harper & Bros., 1858. 732 pages.

Loeb, Jaques. *Comparative Physiology of the Brain and Comparative Psychology*. New York: G. P. Putnam's Sons; London: J. Murray, 1900. 309 pages; illustrated.

Lyon, George Francis. *A Brief Narrative of an Unsuccessful Attempt to Reach Repulse Bay . . . . in the Year 1824*. London: Murray, 1825. Illustrated.

Maine, Sir Henry James Sumner. *Ancient Law: Its Connection with the Early History of Society, and Its Relation to Modern Ideas*. London: Murray, 1901.

Mall, Franklin P. "On Several Anatomical Characters of the Human Brain, Said to Vary according to Race and Sex, with Especial Reference to the Frontal Lobe," *American Journal of Anatomy and Biology*, 1–32. Philadelphia: Thirty-sixth St. and Woodland Ave., 1909.

Martin, Henry Newell. *The Human Body: An Account of Its Structure and Activities and the Condition of Its Healthy Working*. 6th ed., rev. New York: Henry Holt & Co., 1890. 655 pages.

McGhee, Zach. In *Pedagogical Seminary*, VII. No. 4 (December, 1900), 459–91. Clark University, Worcester, Mass. [34]

Middleton, Myres. *The Yahgans—Man*. London, W.: Anthropological Institute, 1902.

Monroe, Will S. "Play Interests of Children," *Proceedings of the N.E.A., 1899*. [35]

Morgan, Lewis Henry. *Ancient Society: Or Researches in the Lines of Human Progress from Savagery, through Barbarism to Civilization*. New York: Henry Holt & Co., 1878. 560 pages. [36]

Mosely Educational Commission to the United States of America, 1903. London: Co-operative Printing Society, 1904. 400 pages.

Murdoch, John. In *American Anthropologist* (1890), 233. Washington, D.C.

————. "East Greenlanders," *American Naturalist*, XXI. Boston. [37]

————. *On the Siberian Origin of Some Customs of the Western Eskimos*. (Pamphlet in Field Museum, Chicago.)

————. In *Popular Science Monthly*, II. New York.

————. In *American Naturalist*, XX and XXXII. Boston, Mass. [38]

————. "Ethnological Results of the Point Barrow Expedition," *Ninth Annual Report of the Bureau of American Ethnology*, 33–441. Smithsonian Institution. Washington: Government Printing Office, 1888. Illustrated. [39]

Murray, John. *A Handbook for Travellers in India, Burma, and Ceylon*. 6th ed. London: Murray, 1907. 524 pages.

Mutch, James S. "Whaling in Ponds Bay," *Boas' Anniversary Volume*, 488. New York: Stechert & Co. 559 pages. [40]

Nelson, E. W. "The Eskimos about Bering Strait," *Eighteenth Annual Report of the Bureau of American Ethnology*, Part I, 3–518. Smithsonian Institution. Washington: Government Printing Office, 1897. Illustrated. [41]

Official Handbook and Catalogue of the Ceylon Courts, 1893.

Ommaney, Sir Erasmus. In *Journal of the Anthropological Institute of Great Britain and Ireland*, XVII. London.

Parry, Wm. Edward. *Journal of a Second Voyage for the Discovery of a Northwest Passage from the Atlantic to the Pacific*. London, 1824. 571 pages; illustrated; 13 maps. [42]

Peary, Robert Edwin. *Northward over the "Great Ice."* New York: F. A. Stokes Co., 1898. 2 vols.; maps. [43]

———. "Journeys in Northern Greenland," *Geographic Journal*, XI.

———. *Snowland Folk*. New York: F. A. Stokes Co., 1904. 97 pages; illustrated.

Peary, Josephine Diebitsch. *The Snow Baby: A True Story with True Pictures*. New York: F. A. Stokes Co., 1901. 8th ed. 84 pages; illustrated.

Peschel, Oscar Ferdinand. *Races of Man and Their Geographical Distribution* (from the German). New York: Appleton, 1900. 528 pages.

Petroff, Ivan. "Alaska, Its Population, Industries, and Resources," *Tenth U. S. Census Report*, VIII, Part I. Washington: Government Printing Office, 1880.

Pinkerton, John. *General Collection of the Best and Most Interesting Voyages and Travels in All Parts of the World*. London: Longman, 1808–14. 17 vols. Illustrated.

Powell, John Wesley. Articles in *Annual Reports of the Bureau of American Ethnology*. Washington: Government Printing Office, 1881–1904.

Rae, ———. *Journal of the Anthropological Institute of Great Britain and Ireland*. London.

———. "Recent Speculations in Primitive Religions," *Review*, XXXVIII, 46.

Rasmussen, Knud. *The People of the Polar North*. Compiled from Danish Originals by G. Herring. Illustrated by Count Harold Molke. London: Kegan Paul, Trench, Truebner & Co., Ltd., 1908. 358 pages. [44]

Ratzel, Friedrich. *The History of Mankind*. Introduction by E. B. Tylor. London and New York: Macmillan, 1896–98. 3 vols.; colored plates, maps, and illustrations.

Reade, William Winwood. *Savage Africa: Being a Narrative of a Tour in Equatorial, Southwestern, and Northwestern Africa*. London: Smith, Elder & Co., 1863. 587 pages; plates, folding map.

Rink, Hinrich Johannes. *Tales and Traditions of the Eskimos, with a Sketch of Their Habits, Religion, Language, and Other Peculiarities*. Edinburgh: Blackwood, 1875. 472 pages. [45]

———. Article on "Eskimos" in *Chambers' Encyclopaedia*, IV, 422. Philadelphia: J. B. Lippincott Co., 1903.

———. *The Eskimo Tribes: Their Distribution and Characteristics, Especially as Regards Language.* London: Williams & Norgate; Copenhagen: C. A. Reitzel, 1887–91. 2 vols. in one; map.

———. Articles in *Journal of the Anthropological Institute,* XVII, 68; also in *Athenaeum,* LXXXVIII.

Rivers, Wm. Halse Rivers. In *Cambridge Anthropological Expedition to Torres Straits.* Cambridge, 1901–8. 3 vols. [45a]

Rivers, Lieut.-Gen. Pitt. In *Journal of Anthropology,* XII, 459.

Ross, Sir John. *Narrative of Second Voyage in Search of Northwest Passage.* Also Appendix. London: A. W. Webster, 1835. [46]

Rotch, Thomas Morgan. *The Hygienic and Medical Treatment of Children.* 3d ed. Philadelphia and London: J. B. Lippincott Co., 1901. 1021 pages.

Rowe, Stewart Henry. *The Physical Nature of the Child and How to Study It.* New York: Macmillan, 1899. 207 pages; bibliography.

Russell, Chas. E. B. *Working Lads' Clubs.* London: Macmillan, 1908. 445 pages.

Sarasin, Dr. Paul and Dr. Fritz. *Die Weddahs von Ceylon.* Wiesbaden: C. W. Kreidel's Verlag, 1893. 599 pages. Also "Atlas." 512–23. [47]

Sauer, Martin. *Account of Geographical and Astronomical Expedition to Northern Parts of Russia, Performed by Commodore Joseph Billings, 1785–94.* London: Cadell, 1802. 332 pages; map. [48]

Schwatka, Frederick. *Children of the Cold.* Boston and New York: Educational Publishing Co., 1902. 212 pages; illustrated. [49]

———. "Explorations," *Science,* II, VI, 172; VII, 172.

Scoresby, William. *Voyage to Greenland.* Edinburgh: A. Constable & Co., 1823.

Seligmann, C. G. "Ceylon: Stone Age," *Man* (May, 1909).

Sheldon, Henry D. "The Institutional Activities of American Children," *American Journal of Psychology,* IX (July, 1898), 425–48. Clark University, Worcester, Mass. [50]

Shinn, Milicent Washburn. *Development of the Senses in the First Three Years of Childhood,* II. Lancaster, Pa.: New Era Printing Co., 1907. 258 pages. [51]

———. *The Biography of a Baby.* Boston and New York: Houghton Mifflin Co., 1900. 247 pages.

Shuttleworth, G. E. *Mentally Deficient Children: Their Treatment and Training.* London: Lewis, 1895. 140 pages. (A new and enlarged edition is being prepared.)

Simpson, Thomas. *Narrative of Discoveries on the Northwest Coast of America.* London: R. Bentley, 1843. 419 pages. [52]

Sisson, Genevra. "Children's Plays," *Studies in Education,* I, 171–74. Edited by Earl Barnes. Leland Stanford Junior University, 1896–97. [53]

Snow, W. Parker. In *Transactions of the Ethnological Society of London.* [54]

Spears, John R. *The Gold Diggings of Cape Horn*. New York: G. P. Putnam's Sons, 1895. [55]

Spencer, Baldwin, and Gillen. *Native Tribes of Central Australia*. London, Macmillan, 1899. 617 pages; illustrated. [56]

Spencer and Gillen. *Northern Tribes of Central Australia*. London and New York: Macmillan, 1904. 784 pages; illustrated. [57]

Spencer, Herbert. *The Principles of Sociology*. 3 vols. New York: Appleton, 1900.

———. *Descriptive Sociology: Or Groups of Sociological Facts*. 8 vols. New York: Appleton, 1873–81. [58]

———. *Education: Intellectual, Moral, and Physical*. New York: Appleton, 1900.

Stewart, Neil Innes. *Manual of Physiology with Practical Exercises*. 5th ed. London: Bailliere, 1906. "University Series." 911 pages; illustrated.

Stow, George W. *Native Races of South Africa: A History of the Intrusion of the Hottentots and Bantu into the Hunting Grounds of the Bushmen*. Ed. by G. M. Theal. London: Sonnenschein. 618 pages. [59]

Tanner, Amy Eliza. *The Child—His Thinking, Feeling and Doing*. Chicago: Rand McNally & Co., 1904.

Thomas, William Isaac. *Sex and Society; Studies in the Social Psychology of Sex*. Chicago: The University of Chicago Press, 1907. 325 pages.

Turner, Lucian M. "Ethnology of the Ungava District, Hudson Bay Territory," *Eleventh Annual Report of the Bureau of American Ethnology*, 159–350. Edited by J. Murdoch. Smithsonian Institution. Washington: Government Printing Office, 1890. [60]

Tylor, Edward Burnett. *Primitive Culture: Researches into the Development of Mythology, Philosophy, Religion, Art, and Custom*. 2 vols. 3d. Am. ed. New York: Henry Holt & Co., 1888. [61]

———. Article on "Anthropology" in *Encyclopaedia Britannica*, II, 115. [62]

Vincent, Frank. *Around and about South Africa*. 5th ed. New York: D. Appleton & Co., 1895. 473 pages.

Waitz, Theodore. *Introduction to Anthropology*. London: Longmans, Green & Co., 1863. 404 pages.

Wallaschek, Richard. *Primitive Music*. London and New York: Longmans, Green & Co. [63]

Warner, Francis. *The Study of Children and Their School Training*. New York and London: Macmillan, 1902. 264 pages; illustrated.

West, Gerald, M. "The Anthropometry of American School Children," *Memoirs of International Congress of Anthropology*. Chicago: Schulte Publishing Co., 1894.

Weddell, James. *A Voyage toward the South Pole*.

Wiedersheim, Robert Ernst Eduard. *Elements of the Comparative Anatomy of Vertebrates*. Adapted from the German by N. W. Parker. 3d ed. London: Macmillan, 1907. 576 pages; illustrated.

Wilkes, Charles. *Narrative U. S. Exploring Expedition*, I, 127. [64]

Williams, Talcott. "Was Primitive Man a Modern Savage?" *Annual Report of the Smithsonian Institution for 1896*, 541–48. Washington: Government Printing Office, 1898.

Wright, G. Frederick. "The Influence of the Glacial Epoch upon the Early History of Mankind," *Records of the Past*, VII, 22–37. Washington, D.C.: Records of the Past Exploring Society, 1908. Illustrated.

Young, Ella Flagg. *Isolation in the School*. Chicago: The University of Chicago Press, 1901. 111 pages.

STUDIES IN PLAY AND GAMES

An Arno Press Collection

Appleton, Lilla Estelle. **A Comparative Study of the Play Activities of Adult Savages and Civilized Children.** 1910

Barker, Roger, Tamara Dembo and Kurt Lewin. **Frustration and Regression: An Experiment With Young Children.** 1941

Brewster, Paul G., editor. **Children's Games and Rhymes.** 1952

Buytendijk, F[rederick] J[acobus] J[ohannes]. **Wesen und Sinn des Spiels.** 1933

Culin, Stewart. **Chess and Playing-Cards.** 1898

Daiken, Leslie. **Children's Games Throughout the Year.** 1949

[Froebel, Friedrich]. **Mother's Songs, Games and Stories.** 1914

Glassford, Robert Gerald. **Application of a Theory of Games to the Transitional Eskimo Culture.** 1976

Gomme, Alice B. and Cecil J. Sharp, editors. **Children's Singing Games.** 1909/1912

Groos, Karl. **The Play of Animals.** 1898

Groos, Karl. **The Play of Man.** 1901

Lehman, Harvey C. and Paul A. Witty. **The Psychology of Play Activities.** 1927

MacLagan, Robert Craig, compiler. **The Games and Diversions of Argyleshire.** 1901

Markey, Frances V. **Imaginative Behavior of Preschool Children.** 1935

Roth, Walter E[dmund]. **Games, Sports and Amusements.** 1902

Sutton-Smith, Brian, editor. **A Children's Games Anthology.** 1976

Sutton-Smith, Brian, editor. **The Games of the Americas, Parts I and II.** 1976

Sutton-Smith, Brian, editor. **The Psychology of Play.** 1976

Van Alstyne, Dorothy. **Play Behavior and Choice of Play Materials of Pre-School Children.** 1932

Wells, H[erbert] G[eorge]. **Floor Games.** 1912

Wolford, Leah Jackson. **The Play-Party in Indiana.** 1959

DATE   DUE

RETURNED NOV 29 '79 UWL	RETURNED UWL
RETURNED	
JUN 1 1987 UWL RETURNED	